JOHN ADAM
The Mulbuie Murderer

D1494534

JOHN ADAM
The Mulbuie Murderer

Graham Clark

UMBRIA PRESS

ISBN: 978 0 9573641 1 0

Umbria Press
London SW15 5DP
www.umbriapress.co.uk

Printed and bound by
Ashford Colour Press, Ltd.
Gosport

Contents

ACKNOWLEDGEMENTS

One of my earliest recollections after my wife and I set up home on the Black Isle was reading an article in the *Inverness Courier* about a plaque that had been erected in a car park to commemorate a murderer named John Adam. Some years later, whilst researching my book *'Redcastle: A Place in Scotland's History'*, I discovered that the victim's corpse had been found close to our Black Isle home. When I also found that both the perpetrator and the victim had originated from my ancestral homelands of Angus and the Mearns, I became obsessed into investigating the whole story. Little did I realise what my subsequent researches would reveal - not only the circumstances of one of Scotland's most notorious murders but a trail of bizarre events, some repercussions of which still persist to this day – almost 180 years on.

It may be a sad admission but I enjoy visiting archive centres, putting on the white gloves and exploring dusty bundles of old documents. In researching this book I did plenty of that and encountered lots of archivists along the way. Without their knowledge and expertise I would have achieved little, so I wish to thank them collectively for their friendly help and professional advice – especially those in the Highland Archive Centre in Inverness and the National Records of Scotland in Edinburgh where most of the dusty documents pertaining to this fascinating murder are archived.

Historical research is collaborative and rewarding. Encouragement and assistance from friends and colleagues is the norm and many have given generously during the compilation of this book. Although they are too numerous to name, I wish to place on record my sincere thanks to them all. However, there is one who must be named – my wife, Linda. I am at a loss to find adequate words to express my indebtedness to her for the constant support she has given throughout the research, the writing and (most importantly) the proof-reading of this book. Her incisive, yet constructive, criticisms have much improved the text and her artistic talents have been gratefully exploited for the conception and design of the cover.

Graham Clark
April 2013

CHAPTER ONE

John Adam

Like so much of John Adam's life, the exact date of his birth is a mystery. Some sources quote 1 January 1804 – although the event is recorded twice as 4 January 1804 in the old parish registers[1] of Lintrathen parish in the county of Forfarshire, Scotland. The register of births[2] states: *4 January 1804: John, lawful son to John Adam and Betty Chepland in West Campsie, baptised;* whilst the entry in the register of baptisms states: *4 January 1804: John, son to John Adam and Betty Cheapland, Wester Campsie.*

In early-19th century Presbyterian Scotland infant mortality ranged from about 8% in rural areas to 30% in urban areas, so it was quite normal for 'lawful' children [those conceived within their parents' marriage] to be baptised on the day of their birth. This ensured that there would be a Christian burial should the child die in infancy. Despite the uncertainty of the actual birth date, what is certain is that the baptism ceremony would have been carried out at West Campsie by the (then) Lintrathen parish minister, Rev George Louden.

Forfarshire was the previous name of the county now known as Angus – supposedly after Oengus, said to have been one of the original mormears of the Pictish kingdom of Alba. In recorded history, the mormeardom of Angus dates from the early-10th century from which it became an early medieval sherrifdom and subsequently an earldom from the mid-13th century. The term 'Forfarshire' became

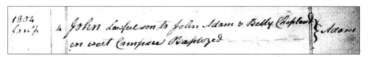

Figure 1: John Adam's baptism record in the Lintrathen old parish register of January 1804 (reproduced with permission of the Church of Scotland)

well-established by the 14th century, although the term 'Angus-shire' is found on 17-18th century maps, suggesting that the original name had remained in local use well before its official re-adoption in 1928.

The rural parish of Lintrathen lies in the foothills of the Grampian mountains in the far west of Angus. The only village in the parish, little more than a hamlet, is Bridgend of Lintrathen, where there is a bridge over the Melgam Water, the river that outflows from the Loch of Lintrathen, and where the parish 'kirk' [the term used for all Scottish Presbyterian churches] is located. The remainder of the parish comprises agricultural settlements (or fermtounes), where the tenant farmers and their workers originally lived but whose cottages are now derelict or have been converted to commuter or retirement houses. The nearest towns are Alyth, five miles to the south-west across the county border in Perthshire, and Kirriemuir, seven miles to the east, famous as the birthplace of JM Barrie, the creator of Peter Pan.

Much of the parish of Lintrathan lies within the Airlie estate, the historic land of the Earls of Airlie. Their ancient stronghold, Airlie Castle, was built by Walter Ogilvy of Lintrathen, Lord High Treasurer of Scotland, on lands granted in 1432 by King James I of Scotland. It stands at the confluence of the Melgam Water and the River Isla, and became the chief residence of the Ogilvies. James Ogilvy was created the 1st Earl of Airlie by Charles I at York in 1639, but his castle was captured and sacked in 1640 when it was attacked by 4000 of Cromwell's parliamentarian troops led by the Earl of Argyll, an incident which is described in the ballad *The Bonnie Hoose o' Airlie*. The 4th Earl of Airlie fought in the Jacobite rebellion of 1745 and had to flee Scotland after the Battle of Culloden, the epic finale in which the Duke of Cumberland ended the ambitions of 'bonny' Prince Charles Edward to overthrow the Hanovarian George II and return the Stuarts to the throne of the United Kingdom. Airlie was pardoned in 1778, although the earldom was not recovered until 1826. The castle was never rebuilt but it was replaced in 1793 by a mansion house that incorporated some of the ruins. This house was restored in the 20th century and is still occupied.

John Adam's paternal ancestors were all born and bred on the

Figure 2: West Campsie farm, Lintrathen, Forfarshire – birthplace of John Adam

Airlie estate. His father, John Adam snr (born *circa* 1760) was the tenant farmer of the hill farm of West Campsie – as was his grandfather, also named John Adam (born 1 February 1718) – and his great-grandfather, James Adam (born *circa* 1690). His grandfather's baptism is unusually recorded in the Lintrathen register of births: *James Adam in Wester Campsie had a child irregularly baptised by a Mr Gorrand, called John.*

After the Reformation of 1560-1690, the Act of Parliament that decreed Scotland to be a Presbyterian country was not immediately adopted by everyone. Mr Gorrand would probably have previously been an Episcopalian minister or Catholic priest who had not yet converted to Presbyterianism (or had not proven his qualification to be formally admitted to the Presbyterian ministry) but who still preached, often outdoors, to congregations of followers. Especially in rural areas, properly qualified ministers could be difficult to find. There were also many 'patronage' disputes about whether it was the heritors [the ruling group of principal landowners in a parish] or the Presbytery who had the right to appoint parish ministers. In these circumstances, parents would often prefer the baptism of their children to be carried out by any clergyman rather than none. Presbyteries and Kirk Sessions referred to these clergy as 'malignant' and to their baptisms as 'irregular'.

The reformed Church of Scotland, generally known as the 'Kirk', was initially governed by ordained ministers and lay elders, in a hierarchical series of 'courts' known as Sessions, Presbyteries, Synods and General Assembly. [Synods no longer exist, having been abolished in 1990.] Individual kirks are managed by the Kirk Session, composed of elders and chaired by the parish minister, known as its Moderator. Presbyteries are regional courts, composed of the ministers of the region and elected 'ruling elders', to which the kirk sessions are responsible. The General Assembly is the supreme court of the Church of Scotland. It meets annually, chaired by an annual appointee known as the Moderator of the General Assembly, who serves as the public representative of the Church – but beyond that enjoys no special powers or privileges.

John Adam's great-grandfather's death is recorded in the Lintrathen old parish registers. This is somewhat unusual because, prior to 1855 – when civil registration of births, marriages and deaths by appointed parish Registrars commenced in Scotland – most Scottish parishes only recorded baptisms and marriages. However the old parish registers of Lintrathen (which commence in 1717) are exceptional because they do record some deaths – or more accurately, they record the rent of a mortcloth. [A mortcloth was a black, usually velvet, piece of cloth that was owned by the parish and could be hired to cover the coffin at a funeral. Sometimes, if a coffin was too expensive, the mortcloth simply covered the body, wrapped in a linen sheet.] On 20 April 1760 an entry in the register of deaths states: *Given in for the use of the mortcloath to James Adam in Campsey, two shillings sterling.*

John Adam also had several uncles and great uncles who were tenant farmers in the area, for example at North Campsie, Clintlaw and Bottom. An entry in the Lintrathen register of deaths/burials on 1 March 1721 refers to one of these ancestors: *Given in for use of the mortcloth to John Adam in Bodam his corps, twenty shills Scots.* Thus, for several generations the extended Adam family had been well-respected church-going members of the Lintrathen community. However, despite their status, the extended Adam family were not rich. Only two of them had ever been of sufficient wealth to register wills – John Adam in Klinthy [Clintlaw] in 1683 and William Adam in

Bottom in 1799. Their wills are recorded in the Register of Testaments of the Commissariot of St Andrews[3].

In Scotland, before 1868, it was not possible to bequeath immoveable heritable property [land and/or buildings] because it automatically passed to the eldest son by the right of male primogeniture [the right of the first-born son to inherit the entirety of his parent's title and estate]. In consequence, only the rich needed to prepare a will or appoint an executor to make an inventory of their moveable property [money or possessions] so that it could be distributed as they wished after their death. Inventories, with or without a written will, were called 'testaments' and they had to be registered with the regional Commissary Court [until 1823, after which Sherriff Courts became responsible]. Other people had little moveable property and it was customary for the immediate family to divide it up as amicably as possible without any formal legal process.

John Adam's testament registered in 1683 was a 'testament testamentar' because it contains a will drawn up by him, in which he describes how his moveable property should be divided between his wife, Isobel Gibbon, and his brother, Andrew Adam. In the case of William Adam in 1799 there was no will, so the Commissary Court appointed Margaret Lindsay as his executrix. She had little to do because William's only substantive possessions were four stacks of oats and bere [barley]. She sold these by public roup [auction] and realised £26-2-11d, which sum of money became the only item in the inventory of William's moveable property [called a 'testament dative' when the executor was appointed by the Court]. It does not seem to be recorded how William's money was distributed – in her role as executrix, Margaret would have offered advice but the decision would have been made by the Court.

The ancestry of John Adam's mother, Betty Chepland, is not known with certainty. If she originated from Lintrathen, her birth was not recorded under that name in the old parish registers. In all probability, she would have been born in circa 1775-80 because her marriage proclamation to John Adam snr is recorded in the Lintrathen parish marriage register on 17 July 1801: *John Adam and Betty*

Chepland both of this parish, gave up their names for proclamation in order for marriage to be proclaimed the three subsequent Sabbaths.

In pre-Reformation Scotland all that was necessary for a marriage to be considered legal was a simple verbal declaration by each of the parties before witnesses. Marriages by 'co-habitation and repute' and by 'betrothal and consummation' were also recognised by Scots law. However, after the Reformation, the Kirk considered such marriages as 'irregular'. For a marriage to be 'regular' it had to take place before an ordained minister following the reading aloud of 'banns' on three Sundays before the marriage ceremony. It is the proclamation of the banns, rather than the marriage itself, that is generally recorded in the old parish registers. Because the banns had to be read in the home parish churches of both parties, there are often two records. Irregular marriages could be regularised (and then registered) by the payment of a fee. Licenses to marry were never issued in Scotland, whilst marriage certificates were only issued after 1855.

John Adam snr and Betty Chepland had five children, all born in West Campsie, Lintrathen: Margaret, the eldest daughter, baptised on 10 June 1802; John, the eldest son, baptised on 4 January 1804; Jannet, baptised on 27 August 1805; James, baptised on 1 May 1807; and William, baptised on 17 January 1811.

Attendance at school in the early-19th century was not compulsory but parish-based education for all children had been a central plank of the Reformation, so most parishes had schools by the early-18th century. Lintrathen was no exception – its 'parochial' school was founded on a site about half a mile south of Bridgend of Lintrathen in 1731. [A new school was built on the same site in 1843 and this still serves as the present school.] No early records of the Lintrathen school have survived, although the kirk session minutes record appointments of some of its teachers [there was generally only one teacher – the headmaster] and some of the annual Presbytery inspections [which determined whether the teachers had performed sufficiently well to actually be paid their annual salaries]. There are also some surviving receipts for the schoolteachers' salaries in the Airlie estate muniments[4] [documents that prove ownership of assets]. For example, the salary receipt for 1814 states: *Received by me, schoolmaster of Lintrathen ... £8-2-6½d being my money salary, including 17/9d allowed for garden ground ... for crop year 1814. (Signed) Mr John Walker.* He also received contributions to his salary from the other estates within the parish in proportion to their size, for example £1-17-1¾d from the Shannally estate.

Part of the schoolteacher's salary was also paid in kind. This was given in proportion to the harvested produce of each farm in the parish. The amount paid in 1814 is not recorded but, for example, in 1803 the teacher's *victual sallary* amounted to 8 bolls, 2 firlots and 3 pecks of oats, of which the Wester Campsie farm was responsible for providing 2 pecks. [A boll was the standard measure of dry volume: 1 chalder contained 8 bolls; 1 boll contained 4 firlots; 1 firlot contained 4 pecks; and 1 peck contained 4 lippies. However, the actual volume differed according to what was being measured. For oats, a boll was about 210 litres, so the teacher was given almost 1800 litres of oats – the value of which, at that time, was about £6.]

In the early-19th century children attended school from age 6 to 12. Lessons in reading, writing and religious education were free but fees were charged for other subjects. Poor parents could apply to their kirk session to pay their children's fees, especially if they displayed higher academic ability. John Adam's father was a church elder, so he would have wanted John to do well at school, especially in winter when there was less need for children to do farm work. West Campsie farm lay only one mile south of the school, so John would readily have walked there.

According to an account[5] provided by Rev Francis Cannan, the Lintrathen parish minister in 1836: *From his childhood up to the nineteenth year of his age, he [John Adam] was generally considered mild, peaceable, obliging, merry, free from malice, honest, forgiving, and not addicted to swearing or intemperance. Although he showed no contempt for religion, he did not evince any sense of religious obligation. He attended church regularly, and about his nineteenth year became a communicant ... almost the only failing, besides his religious indifference, for which he was noted, was a constant practice*

of concealing the truth, when it affected him, and of fabricating lies.
Of John's schooldays, Rev Cannan continued: *He was at school for several years, but showed great disinclination to learn; he frequently remained away many days without the permission of his parents, and was very much in the practice of inventing false excuses, to escape the lash of the teacher. If he was guilty of doing any thing contrary to the rules of the school, he never failed to put the blame on some other person.* So John was a regular truant, never a willing learner and, at an early age, adept at fabricating falsehoods. His skills in concocting plausible, but fictional, stories would be put to regular use in his future life.

Shortly after John completed his schooling in about 1816, his father fell ill and later died. Although the Lintrathen old parish registers did record some deaths, there is no record of John's father's death. This is because there are no surviving death records for the period 1793-1820, the time during which John's father can be assumed to have died, probably in circa 1817-18. Also, as an elder of the kirk, John's father would certainly have been buried in the graveyard of Lintrathen parish church but there are no written records and there is no known, or still readable, memorial stone[6].

After the death of her husband at West Campsie, Betty, John's widowed mother, was given the tenancy of the adjacent smaller farm of Craigieloch. Like West Campsie, Craigieloch farm had been in existence for a considerable time. The earliest reference to Campsie is found in the Airlie estate muniments[4] of 1382 which refer to the *redemption of the lands of Camsy* and there are letters dated 1526 recording the *reversion of the half lands of Campsye, presently occupied by James of Spalding, for 160 merks Scots.* There is also a charter of 1539 in favour of James, Lord Ogilvy, which refers to the *lands of Campsy with grain and fulling mills [cloth, probably linen, processing mills].* The same 1539 charter offers the first record of Craigieloch, referring to the *lands of Cragyloch.* Both farms are marked on Timothy Pont's map of Middle Strathmore 1583-96 – named as W. Kampsy and Kragyloch. Craigieloch is also marked on William Roy's military map of 1750 – named as Craigloch[7].

Figure 3: Lintrathen parish as shown on Timothy Pont's 1583-96 map of Middle Strathmore (reproduced by permission of the National Library of Scotland)

As the eldest male child of the family, John, from the age of about fifteen, helped his mother to raise his younger siblings and to run the farm at Craigieloch. However, as noted by Rev Cannan[5]: *A new era in his life commenced when he [John] was about nineteen or twenty. His passion for women began to show itself in the most violent manner.* He took to wandering away from the farm to socialise with the local girls in the evenings and returning so late at night that he often lay in bed until 12 or 1 o'clock the following day. In consequence, the productivity of the farm declined over the next few years but, fortunately, John's younger brother, James, was showing much more interest in farming and, in effect, was gradually superseding John at Craigieloch.

In 1825 John took up work as a ploughman for Mr George Crichton, at Newbarns farm in the parish of Oathlaw, near Kirriemuir. John had developed, in the words of Rev Cannan[5]: *a most uncommon faculty of flattering and deceiving the female sex ... conduct so generally disapproved of by the grave and decent part of the community, that he considered it necessary to leave the parish.* In effect, John had been banished or 'encouraged to leave' and his new employment would have been arranged to ensure his departure.

The magnitude of his misbehaviour became clear on 5 February 1826 when the minutes of Lintrathen kirk session[8] recorded: *Compeared [summoned] Margaret Ogilvy, confessing herself guilty of fornication with John Adam in Craigyloch. As she cannot speak – her confession was made by signs which her father and mother (being present) pretended to explain. The Session ordered the said John Adam to be summoned to appear before them next Sabbath.* Margaret Ogilvy, born in Lintrathen and baptised on 23 June 1805, was John's cousin and was 20 years of age.

John refused to travel from Oathlaw to comply with the summons and on 20 February 1826 Lintrathen kirk session recorded: *The before named John Adam having been summoned to appear before this Session to answer to the allegations given in by the before named Margaret Ogilvy, failed to appear, notwithstanding having been summoned three times. The Session advised the Minister to write to the Rev Lewis Littlejohn, Minister of Othla [Oathlaw], where the said John Adam now resides to summon him before their Session and to report.*

The kirk session of Oathlaw parish met on 11 March 1826. Their minutes[9] record: *Compeared John Adam who having been cited to attend in consequence of a letter from Mr Louden, Minister of Lintrathen, to answer a charge brought against him by Margaret Ogilvy in that parish – after being suitably admonished and being dealt with to be ingenuous to tell the truth, he denied being the father of the said Margaret Ogilvy's child and was dismissed with repeated admonitions not to aggravate his sin, if guilty, by denial. Clerk was instructed to send an extract of this minute to the Kirk Session of Lintrathen.* As instructed, an extract was sent to Lintrathen kirk session. It reads: *Oathlaw 26 March 1826. The Kirk Session being met and constituted sederunt [quorate], the Moderator compeared John Adam having been cited to attend on consequence of a letter from the Rev George Louden, Minister of Lintrathen, to answer to a charge brought against him by Margaret Ogilvy living in that parish. After being suitably admonished and dealt with to be ingenuous and*

tell the truth, he denied being the father of the said Margaret Ogilvy's
pregnancy. He again being admonished not to aggravate his sin if
guilty by denial was dismissed. The Clerk was instructed to send an
extract of this minute to the Kirk Session of Lintrathen.

Margaret Ogilvy gave birth to a daughter on 25 June 1826, two days after her twenty-first birthday. She is recorded twice in the Lintrathen old parish registers[2]. The register of births states: *25 June 1826. Hellen, daughter in fornication to Margaret Ogilvy (lawful daughter to John Ogilvy, Lochside). She gave up John Adam in Craigyloch as the father of her child, who continues to deny the charge. The child was baptised. The aforesaid John Ogilvy was sponsor for the child.* The register of baptisms records: *25 June 1826. Hellen, daughter in fornication to Margaret Ogilvie (a dumb person). She (by signs) named as father John Adam, Craigyloch, he denied. Her father sponsor.* [Illegitimate children without a named father were not normally baptised at birth. However, they could be if a relative (in this case John Ogilvy, the child's grandfather) promised 'sponsorship' to ensure that the child was brought up in the Christian faith.]

The reason why John should deny being the father of Margaret Ogilvy's child is unclear. Perhaps he sensed that because Margaret was unable to speak she could never prove the accusation or perhaps Margaret's father's willingness to sponsor the child, may have unburdened John from the need to confess. Also, in reality, John may have thought that he had simply continued a well-established family tradition. The inter-related Ogilvy and Adam families of Lintrathen were no strange bed-fellows. For example, in 1821 the kirk session minutes record two such instances. On 11 March, James Adam of Bottom farm was found guilty of fornication with an un-named female and *after professing his sorrow and paying the usual penalty to the Poor's funds was absolved of his sin.* [The penalty for illicit sexual intercourse in the 19th century varied from parish to parish and is not always recorded. It was commonly up to 20/- but this could be mitigated, often to 6/8d, if the couple had subsequently married.] Three months later, on 14 June 1821, Jannet Ogilvy is recorded as having been compeared to the Lintrathen kirk session and found

Figure 4: Craigieloch farm, Lintrathen, Forfarshire

guilty of *antenuptial [pre-nuptial] fornication with James Adam, her husband, who confessing sorrow for said sin was gravely rebuked and exhorted to repentance before the Session and absolved.*

Margaret Ogilvy was not the only girl who had succumbed to John Adam's peccadilloes. On 23 April 1826 the minutes of Lintrathen kirk session record: *Compeared Betty Esson confessing herself guilty of fornication with John Esson [sic, should read Adam] residing at Newbarns in the parish of Othley [Oathlaw] and that the same John Adam is the father of her pregnancy. After a suitable rebuke she was dismissed at present. After which the said John Adam compeared and acknowledged that he was the father of the said Betty Esson's pregnancy who being solemnly rebuked for said sin and exhorted to repentance was absolved.*

Both John Adam and Betty Easson (who was only 16 years old and known as 'Biddy') were further summoned to attend the kirk session for second rebukes. On 18 June 1826 the minutes state: *Compeared Betty Esson guilty of fornication with John Adam as mentioned in minute of 2 April last [sic, should read 23 April] confessing sorrow for said sin, she was again rebuked and seriously exhorted to repentance and absolved.* Five weeks later, on 23 July 1826, the minutes state: *Compeared John Adam, mentioned in minute of 23 April last acknowledging himself guilty as mentioned in the aforegoing minute. He was gravely rebuked and exhorted to repentance for said sin and absolved.*

Biddy Easson's child was born on the same day as John received his second rebuke. The birth is recorded twice in the Lintrathen old parish registers[2]. The register of births states: *23 July 1826. John, son to John Adam in Craigyloch and Bettey Eason. Baptised*; whilst the register of baptisms states: *23 July 1826. John, son to John Adam (the above) in fornication and Betty Eason, Campsie.* The inclusion of the phrase 'the above' is a reference to the preceding entry in the baptism register. It is the entry for Margaret Ogilvy's daughter. John Adam, perhaps, has a unique record of having two children, Hellen and John jnr, born of different mothers, consecutively entered in the birth and baptism registers. According to Rev Cannan[5]: *the children resembled him in a very remarkable way* and it was well-known that *he [John] had intercourse with many other women in the neighbourhood ... and, notwithstanding the injuries he did to many, yet he was more a favourite with the young women of the district than any other person.*

Kirk sessions in the 18th and 19th centuries were fastidious in tracking down the father of an illegitimate child because the mother was a burden on the Poor Funds of the parish if she had no father to provide for the upbringing of the child. John's admission of fatherhood therefore made him responsible for Biddy and John jnr. Burdens of responsibility sat uncomfortably on John's shoulders and he responded in the only way he knew – by absconding.

For the next few years, until 1831, the evidence trail is cold and, therefore, John's whereabouts are not fully established. What is known is that for some period during 1826-31, John was employed as an agricultural labourer at Cairnbank, a magnificent mansion and estate close to the town of Brechin. It was here that he first encountered a lady by the name of Jane (sometimes Jean) Brechin.

CHAPTER TWO

Jane Brechin

Jane Brechin was considerably older than John Adam. The old parish registers of Ecclesgreig[10] (now known as St Cyrus) in the county of Kincardineshire, record her baptism by Rev William Walker: *22 August 1788. Robert Brechin and Jane Falconer in Upper Craighill had a daughter baptised, named Jane – witnesses Alexander Gardyne and Robert Burness.*

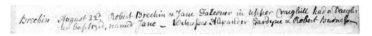

Figure 5: Jane Brechin's baptism record in the Ecclescraig (St Cyrus) old parish register of August 1788 (reproduced with permission of the Church of Scotland)

The old county of Kincardineshire, sometimes called 'The Mearns', lay between the counties of Forfarshire (Angus) and Aberdeenshire [and was amalgamated into Aberdeenshire in 1974]. Upper Craighill and its substantial steadings and farm workers' cottages, still extant today, was a hill farm located in the south of Kincardineshire, 1½ miles north-west of the village of St Cyrus, a fishing village lying on the North Sea coast between the ports of Stonehaven and Montrose. The farmhouse lies at the foot of Woodstone Hill, a probable Pictish hill fort. However, Upper Craighill was not part of the Woodstone estate but of the relatively small neighbouring estate of Criggie, an estate that has existed since 1357 and was owned from 1787 until 1816 by Charles Scott, an Edinburgh JP. He completely renovated the estate, building a new house that was described by George Robertson in 'A general view of Kincardineshire or The Mearns', published in 1813, as: *an elegant modern edifice ... beautifully embosomed amidst young plantations ... a great ornament to this part of the country.*

William Roy's military map[7] of 1750 names *Craigy* and shows an un-named settlement in the location of Upper Craighill. William Garden's 1797 map of Kincardineshire[11] also shows, but does not name, the farm of Upper Craighill. However, it outlines the boundaries of the Criggie estate and names the *Criggie* mansion house and *Upper Criggie* farm. [On modern maps Criggie is now named as Ecclesgreig, the original name of the parish of St Cyrus.]

Jane's father, Robert Brechin, was born on 4 August 1762 in Montrose where the old parish register of births[12] records: *John Brechin and Katherine Robert had a lawful son baptised named Robert, Provost Bisset and John Walker witnesses.* By the time he was nineteen years of age, he was working as an agricultural labourer at Upper Craighill. His marriage contract with Jane Falconer is recorded in the St Cyrus marriage register: *7 September 1782. Contracted Robert Brechen and Jane Falconer, both of this parish.* Jane's paternal grandfather, John Brechin, originated from the adjoining parish of Garvock, where the old parish register[13] of births records: *20 March 1734. John Brechin, son to John Brechin and Ann Hampton* – notably, neither 'lawful' nor 'baptised'. [Garvock is a very rural inland parish bordering St Cyrus. It consists entirely of farms, having no significant village or hamlet.]

Jane's paternal great-grandfather was born in the parish of Marykirk, which borders both St Cyrus and Garvock in the south of Kincardineshire. The baptism register[14] for 16 March 1704 records: *Baptised John Brichan [sic] lawful son to Robert Brichan and Elizabeth Collier in Pittgarvie.* Like Criggie, **Pitgarvie** is named on William Garden's 1797 map of Kincardineshire[11] and on modern maps. Interestingly, two other 'Brichan' baptisms were recorded in Marykirk parish in 1704 – the parents of one of them were George Brichan and Issobell [sic] Hampton, suggesting a certain amount of inter-marrying between the Brechin and Hampton families. The evidence is therefore very strong that Jane's paternal ancestors had been itinerant agricultural workers in the south of Kincardineshire for many generations.

Figure 6: St Cyrus and Criggie as shown on William Garden's 1797 map of Kincardineshire (reproduced by permission of the National Library of Scotland)

Young agricultural workers were commonly referred to as 'agricultural labourers' [often abbreviated to 'ag labs']. They often moved from farm to farm on an annual basis, being hired for the season by tenant farmers, or their grieves [managers or factors], at annual 'feeing' fairs held in local towns [in the case of the Brechin family, probably at the St James's Fair which was held on the Hill of Garvock and was one of the largest annual feeing markets in the area.] 'Ag labs' commonly lived in communal farm 'bothies' but, once married, they sought promotion to more specialised posts, eg cattlemen or ploughmen, and tended to settle and raise their families in rented farm cottages, when they became known as 'cottars'.

Jane Brechin's mother, Jane Falconer, was born on 6 February 1761 in Garvock parish. Her baptism is recorded in the Garvock old parish birth register[13]: *February 6th 1761: Jean Falconar, lawfull daughter to David Falconar and Helen Alexander in St Cyrus baptised before witnesses.* Her parents' marriage is recorded in the Garvock old parish marriage register: *June 13th 1756 David Falconar and Helen Alexander, both in this parish, contracted in order to marriage and married July the 17th.*

Jane Brechin would have been born in one of the farm workers' cottages at Upper Craighill, as would her three siblings: Agnes, baptised 15 July 1783; Robert, baptised 9 May 1785; and Mary, baptised 13 February 1796. However, the family appears to have moved out of Ecclesgreig (St Cyrus) parish shortly after the birth of the youngest child, Mary. In 1799 Rev James Trail, the Ecclesgreig parish minister, drew up a census of all the 1,675 inhabitants living in parish over the period 25 Oct 1798 to 11 Apr 1799. The names are listed in the Ecclesgreig (St Cyrus) kirk session minutes[15] but the Brechin family are not included. It can be inferred that prior to 1798-99 Jane's father had moved the family to a farm in a neighbouring parish. This was probably Garvock parish where Agnes (1806), Robert (1809) and Mary (1822) all married.

In rural areas like Kincardineshire, education was not generally considered a priority for young girls, who from an early age were often required to help their mothers in the house, thus learning domestic skills 'on the job'. If Jane Brechin attended school in the

Figure 7: Farm cottages at Upper Craighill farm, St Cyrus, Kincardineshire – birthplace of Jane Brechin

period 1793-1800, she would initially have attended the parochial school in St Cyrus. A new school had been built in 1782 and was located in the village of St Cyrus, where Joseph Tod was the head teacher. Thereafter she would likely have transferred to the parochial school at Garvock, where Alexander Duncan was the head teacher.

According to most accounts, Jane initially went into service as a maid with various householders in the area around south Kincardineshire and north Forfarshire (Angus). In the late-18th and early-19th centuries young girls of agricultural stock, on leaving school at age 12, had little alternative but to remain at home or go into service as a domestic servant. Whilst offering a wage, the latter option could be dangerous and insecure. A trivial offence could bring instant dismissal without references and pregnancy by the master of the house, or his sons, was a common fate. However, Jane was diligent and hard-working, so she gained good references and gradually rose into employment in the mansions of some local estate owners. It was whilst working as an assistant cook at Cairnbank, near Brechin that she met John Adam.

The small town of Brechin is in north-east of Angus, close to the Kincardineshire border. It was an ancient royal burgh and traditionally is described as a 'city' because its cathedral was the seat of a pre-reformation Roman Catholic diocese. The cathedral is well-known for its 11th century Irish-style round tower, one of only two in Scotland, and its 13-14th century western tower and processional door. Along with the cathedral and round tower, the town also boasts a surviving wall from the chapel of a 13th century *Maison Dieu* [hospital].

The estate known as Cairnbank (and now known as Templewood) originated from the two adjoining estates of Bothers and Templehill. In the late medieval period, Bothers was owned by Brechin Cathedral and Templehill was owned by the Knights of the Order of St John of Jerusalem (Knights Templers). The estates became conjoined in 1587 under the ownership of Robert Kynneir – a powerful landowner who, like many others during the Reformation, employed skilful lawyers to manipulate the transfer to themselves of the pre-Reformation church's land.

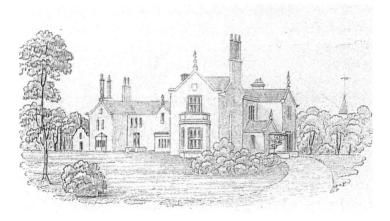

Figure 8: Cairnbank House, near Brechin, Forfarshire (sketch from *Forfarshire Illustrated* 1848)

Cairnbank remained in the Kinnear family for another 100 years. It then passed to various owners until being purchased in 1820 by William Smart. There is a sketch of Cairnbank[16] in *Forfarshire Illustrated*; externally, it has changed little to this day.

William Smart was the son of Robert Smart, a successful merchant from Braehead of Marykirk in Kincardineshire, and Elizabeth Stuart, also from Marykirk parish. William's baptism is recorded in the Marykirk old parish birth register[14], the ninth of twelve siblings born between 1771 and 1795: *February 26th [1786] was baptised William Smart lawful son to Robert Smart and Eliza Stuart in Marykirk, witnesses Alexander Smart and Alexander Boyes*. William married Miss William [sic] Gibson on 23 November 1823 in Montrose. The entry in the Montrose old parish marriage register[12] states: *William Smart Esq and Miss William Gibson, both of this parish were proclaimed in order to marriage and no objections offered*.

Miss William Gibson was a lady of some notoriety, being the woman for whom the lawyer and author George Beattie, best known for his poem *John o' Arnha*, committed suicide. After courting Miss Gibson for some time, George Beattie proposed on 5 May 1823 – a proposal that she accepted. However, three days later she learned that she had inherited a fortune from her uncle in Granada and wrote to George cancelling the engagement, claiming that her mother would never consent to the union. George continued to send letters to Miss Gibson hoping that she would change her mind. However, she did not and George shot himself on the beach at St Cyrus on 29 September 1823. He is buried in the lower churchyard of St. Cyrus parish church where there is a commemorative monument. Miss Gibson married William Smart two months after Beattie's death.

John o' Arnha was actually John Findlay, the Montrose Town Officer during the late-18th and early-19th century. His nickname referred to the hamlet of Arnhall [in north Angus], where he was born. Findlay was very authoritative and always carried a cudgel which he frequently used to control the town's inhabitants. Although he was teetotal, he is best remembered for telling exaggerated and boastful stories, usually in the Star Inn. These inspired George Beattie's comic poem featuring the effect of drink consumed at Montrose's Annual Fair and John's supposed subsequent encounters with witches and other fanciful creatures. Written in the Scots vernacular in the same style as Robert Burns' epic poem Tam o' Shanter, many critics consider Beattie's poem to rate equal to that masterpiece.

William Smart was in partnership with his brothers Alexander and George, in the firm of A W & G Smart, grain merchants in Montrose. The 'Report on the Burgh' that accompanied the publication of the 1832 Great Reform Act plan of the town[17], states that *the most important article of export is grain, which in quantity is said to exceed, and in quality is not surpassed by the export of any other port in Scotland.* William had also purchased shares in several railway companies and owned a number of properties in Angus, including: Cairnbank and Easter Pitforthy in Brechin; Lochlands and Smithycroft in Arbroath; Muirhouse in Inverkeilor; and houses in Castlegate (also known as Castle Street) in Montrose. By virtue of his share earnings and the rentals from his properties, as well as his business interests, William Smart was a very rich and influential man. Accordingly, he was also a Commissioner of Peace for Forfarshire, a turnpike road trustee and a registered parliamentary elector.

Jane Brechin and John Adam probably first met at Cairnbank in 1827. John is said to have initially befriended Jane to get additional food to supplement what would have been his meagre rations in the farm workers' bothy. The friendship seems to have blossomed into a love affair fuelled by Jane's infatuation for the tall and handsome John Adam – to the extent that Jane was teased by her fellow servants for being about to *marry a laddie*. However, for reasons unknown, there was no wedding – and John Adam again took flight.

Several years later, at Whitsunday 1833 [28 May], Jane Brechin left her employment at Cairnbank to open a small grocery shop in Montrose – an extraordinary move for a house servant. It is tempting to speculate that William Smart played some part in this, not only because the shop was in Market Street (where he owned properties) but also because some degree of financial investment would have been required. Jane's income as a cook would have been higher than that of most house servants, so it is possible that she was able to save sufficient money. However, her father had died in about 1820 [there appears to be no record of his death or burial] and her mother had moved to Laurencekirk. As she had little prospect of earning a living and there is no record in the Laurencekirk Poor Roll of her receiving parish assistance, it seems probable that Jane had been financially supporting her out of such savings as she was able to amass.

Laurencekirk is the principal village of the 'The Howe of the Mearns' – the fertile agricultural area in the south-west of the old county of Kincardineshire. Although there had previously been a small settlement known as Kirkton of Conveth on the site, Laurencekirk was founded in 1759 as an industrial 'planned' village. It quickly grew to become the market and commercial centre of 'The Mearns' and became a Burgh of Barony in 1779. In 1787 Robert Burns came to Laurencekirk to visit the area where his father was brought up before moving to Ayrshire. Another famous son of 'The Mearns' was the author Lewis Grassic Gibbon who wrote about the area in his trilogy entitled *A Scots Quair* and, in particular, the first book *Sunset Song*, written in 1932.

What seems possible is that, as a reward for years of loyal service,

William Smart may have requested Jane to open a small retail outlet for some of the produce from the Cairnbank farm. [It is worth noting that William Smart appears to have been a man who rewarded good employees; for example, when he died (on 24 September 1853) he bequeathed[3] £100 to his long-serving head cook, Jean Buchan.] Setting up such retail outlets seems to have been normal practice by the landowners in and around Montrose, as illustrated in a petition recorded in the minutes of Montrose Burgh Council[18] in December 1833: *Various merchants and guild brethren in the Burgh complaining of their privileges as Burgesses and Guild Brethren being violated by an establishment recently opened in Mill Street under the name of William Matthew for the sale of grocery goods.* Jane's grocery may have been established by William Smart as part of a concerted effort by local landowners to put William Matthew out of business.

Whatever the reason for its establishment, Jane made a considerable success of her business. On 8 April 1834 she deposited £15 into the National Bank of Scotland (receiving a deposit receipt numbered 6/526); and on 3 June 1834 she deposited £96 into the British Linen Bank in Montrose (receiving a deposit receipt numbered 150). The spending power of £96 in 1834 was equivalent to about £8,000 today.

Figure 9: Receipt for £96 deposited by Jane Brechin in the Montrose branch of the British Linen Bank in June 1834 (National Records of Scotland)

CHAPTER THREE

Dorothy Elliott

John Adam left Cairnbank in 1827-28, probably to escape Jane Brechin's desire to marry him. For the next two or three years there is little evidence of his whereabouts. He seems to have been mostly in Aberdeenshire, where he is said to have met up with 'kindred spirits' and to have lived on the proceeds of occasional farm work and petty theft. However, there is no record of him facing trial for theft in Aberdeen Sheriff Court or having received a summary conviction by the Sheriff (which became possible from 1828)[19]. Some later reports suggest that he spent time in Lanarkshire but there is no tangible evidence for this.

There is a story about a remarkable incident that John Adam subsequently related on several occasions. If it contains any element of truth, it probably occurred during his sojourn in Aberdeenshire. He claimed to have met and befriended a young woman with whom he was soon engaged to be married. However, a few days before the date of the wedding, John had a dream that his fiancée had stood at the foot of his bed and had spoken these words: *John, we shall never be married – but mark, you will die an awful death.* On the next evening John walked to his fiancée's house. As he approached in the twilight he could hear the sounds of psalms being sung and, on reaching the window, could see a corpse laid out on a bed surrounded by the worshippers. The corpse was that of his intended bride who had suddenly died that morning!

Whilst in Aberdeenshire, the 'religious indifference' of John's youth is said to have developed into an involvement in Deism – a set of beliefs in which he retained a genuine lifelong interest. [Deists believe that God, having configured the natural world at the creation, does not now intervene with it – allowing it to run entirely according to the laws of nature. This belief took hold during the 17th century 'scientific revolution' and the 18th century 'enlightenment' when Deism became a significant influence in religious thinking. One of its main protagonists was Thomas Paine who wrote *The Age of Reason* in 1794 in which he argued against institutionalized religion and advocated deism by virtue of reason and freethinking. As a consequence of their views, Deists consider it unnecessary to have 'faith' to believe in God, thus they do not accept any of the ceremonies of the Christian faiths.]

What is certainly known about John Adam's time in Aberdeenshire is that in 1830 he was living at Blairdaff in the parish of Chapel of Garioch. There, on 15 August 1830, the Treasurer of the kirk session noted in his accounts[20]: *John Adam and Janet Laing paid their penalty of £1-0-0.* The reason for the fine [sometimes referred to as 'buttock-mail'] became clear almost three months later when the old parish register of baptisms[21] recorded: *John Adam in Blairdaff had a son born of Janet Laing an unmarried woman in Bogranie on 3rd of November 1830, baptised on the 12th of said month and named John in the presence of Alexander Laing and William Duncan both in Bogranie.* Once again, John was soon to take flight from one of his frequent entanglements and from any responsibility for his new-born child. On this occasion he headed for Glasgow, where he enlisted in the Army on 7 January 1831.

The Regiment that John joined was the 2nd (or Queen's) Dragoon Guards[22]. Standing 6ft 1in [185 cm] tall, he must have made a fine guardsman and his farm upbringing would have endowed him with skill in handling horses. However, there is more than a hint that joining the Army was not just an attempt to escape from his past but was also designed to make him almost untraceable. Although he informed the Army of his birthplace correctly, he provided as his next-of-kin a so-called brother named Isaac Adam, whom he stated was a resident of the parish of Kirkintilloch, Lanarkshire. [This Army record may be the origin of the reports that John had spent time in Lanarkshire during 1827-30. However, the town of Kirkintilloch is actually in Dunbartonshire and no Isaac Adam is recorded in any of the old parish registers or in the 1841 national census – nor is there any record of a birth in Lintrathen.]

John was initially stationed in Manchester with the 2nd Dragoon Guards – and then in Leeds, where he spent sixteen days in hospital during September and October 1831, although there is no specific illness or injury recorded. He was subsequently billeted in York until 31 March 1832. The Regiment then marched for thirteen days to reach Edinburgh where it was stationed throughout the next year until 31 March 1833. John was given leave for the first two weeks of November 1832 during which he visited his mother, Betty, and brother, James, at Craigieloch farm. On that visit he also seems to have rekindled his liaison with Jane Brechin, who at that time was still at Cairnbank. The evidence comes from Jane's cousin, William Barclay, a shoemaker who had a shop in Castle Street, Montrose. From time to time, Jane visited William. On one occasion in 1832, she asked William to put an address on a letter. This was because Jane's handwriting, even of her signature, was extremely faltering and barely decipherable. The address on this occasion was John Adam, Private 2nd Dragoon Guards, Capt Smith's Troop, Piercehill Barracks, Edinburgh. The letter contained a proposal from Jane that she purchase John's discharge from the Army – a proposal that William's father had advised against. After that visit, Jane had asked for several other letters to be addressed. Clearly Jane was keen to keep in touch with John – and had lost neither her love for him nor her desire to marry him.

John did not take up Jane's offer of a discharge and the Regiment of the 2nd Dragoon Guards was again on the march from 1 April 1833, this time for nineteen days, to Nottingham. As a private, John's wages (pay and beer money) were 1/4d per day, although he received additional allowance through a voucher scheme whilst on the march. In Nottingham, John was assigned to guard the Law Courts in Derby. Although he was mainly billeted at the Duffield Barracks on the northern outskirts of the city, when the courts were in session he lodged with the proprietor, Ralph Ordish, of the Red Lion Inn, 22 Cornmarket, Derby. It was there that he met and fell in love with a young girl by the name of Dorothy Elliott.

Dorothy lived with her parents in Wirksworth, a town twelve miles north of Derby in the foothills of the High Peak district. In Roman times (and probably before), Wirksworth was an important lead mining and smelting centre and this was still a well-established industry at the time of the Norman Conquest. The mines at Wirksworth are recorded in the

Figure 10: A late-19th century view of the Cornmarket, Derby

Domesday Book and the town paid royalties to the Crown for centuries afterwards. In the 16-18th centuries Wirksworth boomed and became the third most important town in Derbyshire – although its lead mining and smelting industry caused the town severe environmental problems. One observer in the early-19th century described Wirksworth as *eternally overhung by smoke from the lead (and calamine) works*. However, the Derbyshire lead mining industry declined rapidly in the early-19th century with the coming of the Industrial Revolution and the importing of cheaper lead from overseas. The opening up of limestone quarries sustained the town until the mid-19th century but its population fell sharply thereafter. [The fictional village of 'Snowfield' in 'Stonyshire' in George Eliot's first novel *Adam Bede*, published in 1859, is modelled on Wirksworth. The names were derived from the white dust of the lead smelters and the limestone quarries.] Today, Wirksworth is a pleasant small market town with a flourishing tourist trade based on its remarkable industrial heritage.

Although Dorothy Elliott and her parents lived in Wirksworth in the 1830s, they did not originate from Derbyshire[23]. They had come from Northumberland where Dorothy had been born in Longbenton in the coal mining parish of Benton in the north-east of Newcastle-on-Tyne[24]. The birth and baptism are recorded in the register of the non-conformist High Bridge Meeting: *Edward Elliott native of Welton, County of Northumberland, and Margery Herdman native of Thockrington parish same County, his wife, had a daughter born in Benton parish the 8th of June and baptised the 7th of September 1817 – name Dorothy. Witnesses: James Hood; William Wilson & congregation.* [Thockrington is a rural parish about twenty miles northwest of Newcastle and ten miles north of Hexham and Corbridge. Welton is a small village about five miles north-east of Corbridge.]

Edward and Margery had married on 31 July 1813 in Corbridge, Northumberland. They moved to Longbenton in about 1815 and had two daughters: Dorothy, born 8 June 1817 and baptised 7 September 1817; and Jane, born 17 October 1820 and baptised 31 December 1820. Edward's profession is not recorded in the Benton parish birth/baptism registers of either of his daughters but he seems to have been a lead miner, probably employed at the Allenheads Lead Mine close to Longbenton. Sometime in the 1820s Edward moved his family to Wirksworth. Population studies based on 19th century censuses show that the surname Elliott was predominantly found in Northumberland and Derbyshire, so Edward may have moved to Wirksworth because he had relatives who could provide him with employment there.

There were hundreds of small lead mines in the Wirksworth area. This is because any man who discovered a significant amount of lead ore could demonstrate it to the 'Barmaster of the Barmote Court' and obtain a licence to open a mine. He could also retain title to the mine as long as he worked it. Lead mining took precedence over land ownership and no land owner could interfere with lead mining. However, mines were not easy to make profitable and many miners had to share the labour and financing with relatives and neighbours. Others became contractors ('copers') or labourers ('hirelings'). Legal jurisdiction over all mining issues, *e.g.* registrations of mines and resolutions of disputes, was the responsibility of the 'Great Barmote Court of the Soke and Wapentake of Wirksworth'. This Court had originally been created by Edward I in 1288 to legislate on his behalf over lead mining matters within the area known as the 'King's Field' (effectively the entire Derbyshire Peak District).

There is no record in the Wirksworth Barmote Court records of Edward Elliott claiming title to any mine. However, in her 1835 testimony, Dorothy Elliott refers to her father being employed as a miner by a person named John Bunting. There are two records of John Bunting serving as a juror for the Wirksworth Barmote Court[25] in October 1827 and May 1828. He owned mines in Bonsall and Matlock [parishes to the north of Wirksworth] and there are also several records of the Bunting family in the birth and marriage records of these parishes. It seems probable therefore that Edward Elliott had become an itinerant 'hireling' who worked for John Bunting (and perhaps others) as required.

John Adam first met Dorothy Elliott on Christmas Day 1833 at the Red Lion Inn in Derby where she worked as an assistant cook. Over the next two months they met on several occasions, especially when John was billeted there. On 18 March 1834, when he was stationed at Duffield Barracks, John made an unexpected visit to Dorothy in Derby. Unusually, he was wearing plain clothes which he told Dorothy was because he had decided to buy his discharge from the Army. He then asked her to accompany him to Scotland, proposing that they get married on the way. Dorothy's parents disapproved but, at John's suggestion, she told them that she was already married to John. A few

Figure 11: Wirksworth, Derbyshire in 1817 (Joseph Farington print)

days later she agreed to go – on the assurance that he would marry her in Sheffield, their intended first destination *en route*.

There was a pressing reason why John had induced Dorothy to elope with him in unseemly haste. He had not purchased a discharge from the Army – he had deserted. The Regiment recorded the desertion date as 18 March 1834 in their pay and muster rolls[22] and issued a Desertion Report[26] (number 12264) from Nottingham on 27 March 1834. This report stated that John was *25 years, looks much older* [actually he was 30] with a fresh complexion, hazel eyes and brown hair – although it notes that he was bald and wore a wig at the time of desertion. The report also stated that he was *suspected to have stolen a considerable sum of money* and was *thought to have gone to Scotland*. These details were entered into the Register of Army Deserters[27] and, in anticipation of John's eventual capture, a reference number (57269) was issued for a subsequent entry into the Register of Captured Deserters[28].

When John and Dorothy reached Sheffield, the promised marriage was postponed on account of there being insufficient time. They proceeded to York where they took the mail coach to Perth via Edinburgh. [Royal Mail coaches began carrying mail and passengers in 1784. By the 1830s inter-city travelling by mail or stage coach had superseded horseback riding.] At Perth they transferred to the Defiance stage coach to Forfar and, finally, they walked the remaining twelve miles to Craigieloch farm in Lintrathen. [The Defiance stagecoach company was founded in 1830 by Robert Barclay Allardice, who was born in 1777 in Stonehaven, Kincardineshire. Commonly known as 'Captain Barclay', he made the Defiance between Edinburgh, Glasgow and Aberdeen the most efficient and reliable stagecoach service in Scotland.] At Craigieloch, Dorothy was introduced to John's mother (Betty), brother (James), and sister (Jannet) as John's wife, although they had not married in the course of their journey as John had promised.

The news of John's homecoming, and his new 'wife', quickly spread. In particular, there was one interested party by the name of Biddy Easson. Biddy was living in Dundee and her illegitimate son, John, was now almost eight years old. The Lintrathen kirk session had heard about John's visit to Craigieloch when on leave from the

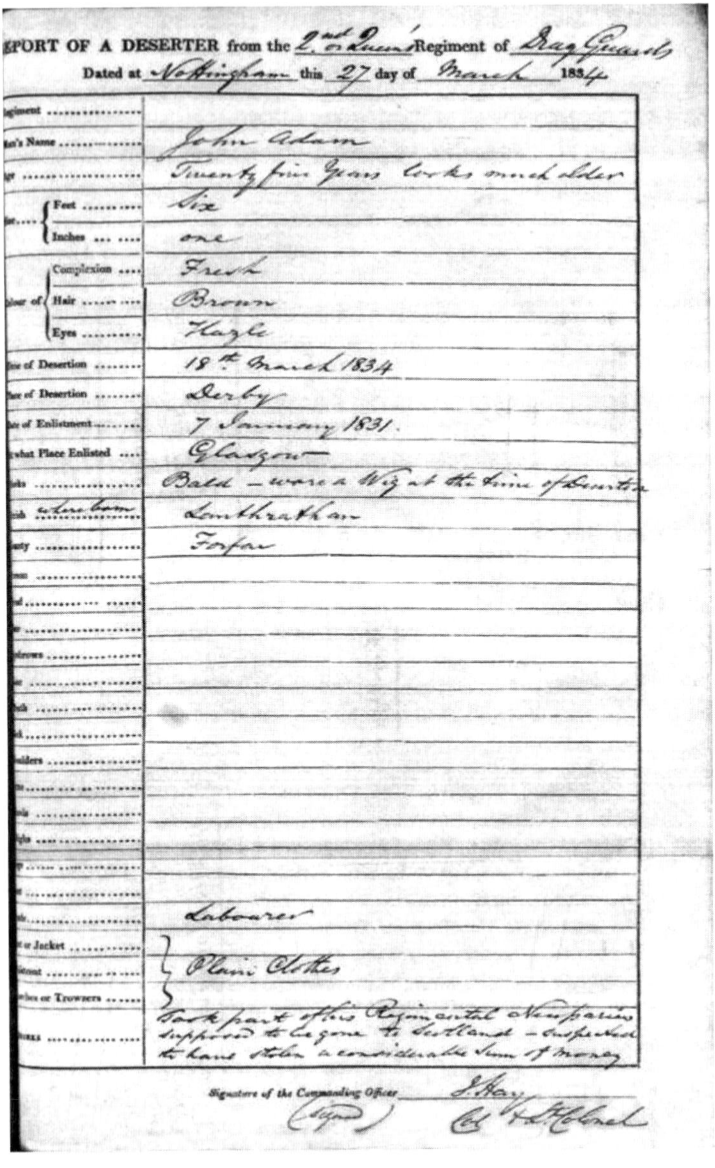

REPORT OF A DESERTER from the *2ⁿᵈ or Queen's* Regiment of *Drag Guards*

Dated at *Nottingham* this *27* day of *March* 1834

Regiment	
Man's Name	John Adam
Age	Twenty five Years looks much older
Size { Feet	Six
Inches	one
Complexion	Fresh
Colour of { Hair	Brown
Eyes	Hazle
Time of Desertion	18ᵗʰ March 1834
Place of Desertion	Derby
Date of Enlistment	7 January 1831
At what Place Enlisted	Glasgow —
Marks	Bald — wore a Wig at the time of desertion
Parish where born	Lentrathan
County	Forfar
Trade	Labourer
Coat or Jacket	} Plain Clothes
Waistcoat	
Breeches or Trowsers	
Remarks	Took part of his Regimental Newspapers supposed to be gone to Scotland — suspected to have stolen a considerable Sum of money

Signature of the Commanding Officer *J. Hay*
(signed) *Lt Colonel*

Figure 12: Report of John Adam's desertion from the 2nd Dragoon Guards in March 1834 (National Records of Scotland)

Army in 1833 and, determined to make John contribute to his son's upbringing, had contacted Dundee (General) kirk session[29]. Their minute of 20 November 1833 states: *Extract from the Session of Lintrathen was read stating that Miss Easson belonging to that parish had been guilty of a relapse* [sic] *of fornication and was now living in this parish, and authorising the Session here to do in the matter as they see most for edification. Compeared Elizabeth Easson unmarried, confessed having brought forth a child named as the father John Adams also unmarried now in the Army. Send entrant to Lintrathen.*

The Lintrathen kirk session would probably have received the response from Dundee before John and Dorothy's visit to Craigieloch in March/April 1834. However, it was not until 4 May 1834 that it was recorded[8]: *Compeared Betty Eason mentioned in a preceding minute and produced a Certificate that she had judicially confessed before the Kirk Session of Dundee and as John Adam had confessed that he was the father of her child, she was rebuked and admonished and restored to Church privileges.* One privilege in which Biddy was particularly interested was that she could now request the kirk session to pursue John Adam on her behalf. This seemed to be a strategy well worth pursuing as John had been telling his friends in Lintrathen that Dorothy was a rich girl who had purchased his release from the Army. To back up this pretence, John had been able to display a degree of wealth by virtue of the money that he had stolen from the Army.

According to a statement made by Rev Cannan[5] in 1836, whilst John Adam was in Lintrathen during March/April 1834 some of Biddy Easson's relations approached him with regard to paying for the maintenance of his child. When he showed no inclination to do so, they petitioned the Sheriff to arrest him. [In Scotland, the 'Sheriff' is the chief law-officer in a shire, responsible to the Crown for peace, civil order and criminal jurisdiction in his area. Deputies, officially called 'Sheriff-Substitutes', perform most of the civil and criminal judicial duties of the office.] On being apprehended, John agreed to pay £20 and have a document drawn up assigning his brother, James, responsibility for the provision of maintenance until the child was able to support himself. However, at the meeting which had been convened to complete the transaction, John tore up the document. Being a Sunday, the Sheriff could not be called until the next day, by which time it was too late – John and Dorothy had left, apparently to catch a stagecoach back to England.

They had stayed in Lintrathen only eight days. Not only did John want to escape the attentions of Biddy Easson's family and the Sheriff, he was also concerned that the Army would soon find him if he remained too long in Lintrathen. In fact, the latter concern was well founded. Just two days after he and Dorothy had departed, Rev Cannan received a letter from the War Office informing him that John Adam had deserted and inquiring whether he had been seen in his home parish.

Although John had been receiving letters from Jane Brechin since 1832 and would have known that Jane had now opened her shop in Montrose, it is improbable that Jane would have known that John was in Lintrathen for eight days during March/April 1834. It is even less likely that John would have attempted to meet her. He would not have wished Jane to know about Dorothy – and certainly not that he was married to her, even if he wasn't.

John and Dorothy did not return to England. Instead, they avoided detection by setting off on foot to the north. They travelled light – leaving behind a 'band box' [a light-weight cylindrical box used to carry items of clothing]. John also began to use the name of John Anderson, explaining to Dorothy that he had another illegitimate child and was afraid of being tracked. Having been raised in the foothills of the Grampians, John would have been well acquainted with the many mountain tracks and passes in the area. Their route initially took them to Braemar (probably crossing the mountain area known as the 'Mounth' by the track known as 'Jock's Road'); then to Tomintoul (probably traversing the Cairngorm mountains using the pass known as the 'Lecht'); and, finally, to Inverness (probably over the Cromdale Hills and the Dava Moor or by using the pass known as the 'Slochd'). This route, extending to about 100 miles, was completed in only eight days – not an exceptional walk for the Army-trained John but probably a significant walk for Dorothy, because food and shelter would at times have been difficult to find and, in early April, the higher passes could still have been snow-covered.

Whether John had originally planned to head for Inverness is not clear. More probably he was just putting as much distance as possible between himself and the inevitable pursuit of the Army. As for Dorothy, she must have been puzzled by what had happened to her since agreeing to accompany John out of Derbyshire. He had not married her, as had been promised, and she must have begun to suspect that there were other motives for travelling so far north. However, she did care for him and she did want to marry him, so she was prepared to wait. Anyway, without the means to return south, she had little alternative.

When John and Dorothy left Derby in mid-March 1834, John was carrying £60 in bank notes – although the Army never published the actual amount of money that he had stolen. A month later, having expended on coaches and accommodation in reaching Forfar and having given £20 to the Sheriff for Biddy Easson, by the time they reached Inverness in mid-April he had only £10 remaining. This was in the form of two £5 notes – one from the Nottingham Bank and the other from the Derby Bank. Such banknotes were of no value in Inverness, so John and Dorothy had to stay whilst the National Bank of Scotland branch in Inverness arranged for the notes to be exchanged for two Bank of England notes. This took two weeks, during which they lodged with a Mr Macdonald, an old man who lived at 3 Gordon Place.

With little money left, John spent much of his time in Inverness seeking work. However, with no skill to offer any tradesman, he was advised to seek agricultural labouring work further north in Ross-shire. In particular, he was directed to Major Mackenzie of Fodderty, near Strathpeffer, who was said to be seeking farm labourers. [Major Forbes Mackenzie of Fodderty is famous for finding, in April 1828, one of his fields covered with herring fry. He forwarded a small quantity of the fish to the Secretary of the Northern Institution whose explanation was that the fish had been transported by a waterspout from the Cromarty Firth three miles away.]

As soon as the English banknotes had been exchanged, John and Dorothy took the Kessock ferry across the Beauly Firth and set off over the Black Isle probably towards Alcaig, where there was a passenger ferry over the Cromarty Firth to Dingwall. [The Black Isle, despite its name, is not an island but a small peninsula north of Inverness bounded by the Beauly, Moray and Cromarty Firths.] In Dingwall, using the surname Anderson, they took lodgings with John Urquhart, a sawyer, and his wife, Christian. The exact address is not recorded but the town plan of Dingwall[30], drawn by John Wood in 1821, shows a house at the extreme west end of Main Street occupied by J. Urquhart. The house also seems to be recorded in the Register of Electors of the Burgh of Dingwall, drawn up subsequent to the 1832 Reform Act. This document[31] makes reference to a *Tenement of Houses built on a piece of ground let by Henry Davidson of Tullich to John Urquhart, cooper in Dingwall* – but gives its location only as *a property situated in Dingwall.*

Next day, John met with Major Mackenzie's factor – but he did not take the work on offer at Fodderty because he regarded the wages as being too low. On his way back to Dingwall, he met David Sutherland, who held the tenancy of the Craig Quarry from its owner, Duncan Davidson of Tullich. John was in luck – he was hired at 1/6d per day and started work at the quarry on 4 May 1834. John Adam and Dorothy Elliott, alias Mr and Mrs Anderson, settled down to life in Dingwall.

Figure 13: The Craig Quarry near Dingwall where John Adam worked in 1834-35

CHAPTER FOUR

Two Wives and a Marriage

For much of the summer of 1834, John Adam, alias Anderson, worked at the Craig Quarry, located 1½ miles to the north-east of Dingwall close to the road that follows the shore of the Cromarty Firth towards Foulis Ferry, Invergordon [in the 19th century known as Inverbreakie] and Tain. David Sutherland, the tenant of the quarry, had secured good contracts for building stone that kept the quarry in profitable work. John was a good employee, described by David as *a strong active labourer, very quiet, pleasant and most obliging ... [whom I] ... never saw worse for liquor or utter an oath.*

However, as autumn set in, work at the quarry became slack and John was laid off. He obtained work for the next six weeks with Neil MacNeil, a mason who had purchased stone from the quarry. Thereafter he was re-engaged by David Sutherland at 1/8d per day – but only for days on which the quarry was working. By late autumn there were few working days and the lack of money was becoming a problem for John and Dorothy Anderson.

Dorothy was also becoming increasingly concerned about her status. John had still not made her his 'lawful' wife, using the excuse that *they would not marry him in Dingwall* because neither of them originated from the parish. Becoming unsatisfied with her circumstances, she expressed a wish to return home to her parents. John said that he had tried to borrow money from David Sutherland so that she could return to Derbyshire but he had refused. In reality, David Sutherland had given John £1-3/-, not as a loan but as an advance on wages. John and Dorothy's quarterly rent payment was also due to be paid at Martinmas [28 November]. In desperation, John announced that he would go south to get money from his mother and brother in Lintrathen – and immediately set off.

Two weeks later John returned with money to pay the rent and

19/- which he gave to Dorothy to buy food. He also was fortunate on his return to find that David Sutherland had employment for him in the quarry. This work lasted until mid-January 1835 and provided sufficient extra cash for John and Dorothy to survive the early winter.

It is not known with certainty how John obtained the money that he brought back from his visit to Forfarshire in November 1834. No witnesses refer in later statements to John being in Lintrathen at that time and, in any case, it is unlikely that he would have dared to return to the very place where Biddy Easson, the kirk session and the Army would certainly have been watching for him. In reality, John had travelled to Montrose and the money had almost certainly come from Jane Brechin. She must also have had prior knowledge that he would be visiting Montrose because she had purchased a pair of men's shoes from her shoemaker cousin, William Barclay, in September 1834 and John had worn them during a visit to the Barclay house in November 1834.

Further evidence was soon to emerge that John had stayed with Jane during the fortnight he had been away from Dingwall in November 1834. In early February 1835 a letter arrived at Dingwall Post Office, addressed to John Adam, c/o John Anderson, Dingwall. John had asked at the Post Office on several occasions during January if a letter had arrived for him, so he obviously had been expecting one. When the letter arrived, John told Dorothy that it was from a solicitor to inform him that he had been left a bequest by an uncle who had died in the West Indies – and that he had to go south to collect it. Dorothy, whose level of literacy seems to have been quite low, persuaded John to let her see the letter. She noted that it was postmarked from Montrose on 4 February 1835, but she became suspicious that the poor writing and the apparent contents did not seem to convey the formal notification of a legacy.

In fact, the letter had come from Jane Brechin who had, again, requested a third party to address it. During his visit in November 1834, John had given Jane a sealed letter addressed to Jane's brother-in-law, Archibald Gouk, a farmer who lived on Rossie Island, in the parish of Craig just to the south of Montrose. This letter contained a note of John's address in Dingwall, to which any letter from Jane should be sent: John Adam, c/o John Anderson, Dingwall. In January 1835, when Jane's letter to John was ready to be sent, she sealed it and arranged for her sixteen-year old niece, Mary Gouk, to collect both letters and take them to her father with instructions to open John's letter and write the address it contained on Jane's letter. When the letter had been addressed, Mary then brought the letter back to Jane who took it to the Post Office for despatch. A week later, Mary carried a second letter from Jane to her father to be addressed. John obviously knew that there would be a second letter because he enquired about it at the Post Office in Dingwall on several occasions during early February.

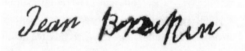

Figure 14: Jane Brechin's signature (National Records of Scotland)

Despite the impending arrival of the second letter, John decided that he had to leave for Montrose immediately. Before leaving, he tried to borrow 5/- from David Sutherland, his employer in the Craig quarry, to help pay for transport. He was given 3/-. A few days later, on 18 February 1835, the second letter arrived at Dingwall Post Office – but John had already departed. Like the previous one, the second letter was addressed to John Adam, c/o John Anderson. As the Post office knew that John was expecting it, the deputy postmistress, Mrs Hay (the postmaster's mother), brought it to Dorothy. However, the postage had not been pre-paid and Dorothy could not afford to pay, so it was placed in the Post Office window, to await collection.

John's story that Jane Brechin's first letter had intimated an inheritance from an uncle in the West Indies was, of course, a fabrication. That letter had been sent for the entirely different purpose of informing John that Jane had sold her shop in Montrose and was now ready to make arrangements for the event that had been planned during John's visit to Montrose two months earlier in November 1834 – their marriage.

During that visit John had promised to marry Jane – perhaps a promise solicited by Jane in return for the rent money. She had been chasing John for six years and was not going to let him go this time. John, on the other hand, had a longer-term plan. He wanted Jane to sell her grocery business in Montrose before marrying and moving to Inverness where, he had told her, he was employed as a sawyer. In the meantime, he would return to Inverness, look for a place where she could open up another shop and await her letter to inform him when she had sold the shop in Montrose.

When John returned to Montrose in mid-February 1835, one of the first things that he did was to send a Postal Order for 20/- to Dorothy – an interesting gesture, given that his purpose for being in Montrose was to marry Jane, from whom he had presumably obtained the money to purchase the Postal Order. It was sent in a pre-paid letter and Dorothy immediately cashed it to buy food. [Postal Orders were first introduced by private banks in 1792. In the early-19th century they were adopted as a means by which money orders could be purchased and redeemed in Post Offices.] The money must have been desperately needed, as evidenced in the Dingwall kirk session poor roll account[32] of February 1835 which itemises a payment of 5/- made to *Mrs Anderson from the South*.

Since opening her grocery business in May 1833, Jane had lived in the backroom of the shop in Market Street. When he arrived in Montrose in February 1835, John moved in with her. However they soon had to vacate because Jane's lease of the premises was due to end at Candlemas [the original Christian festival was held forty days after Christmas on 2nd February but in Scotland the 'quarter day' is fixed at 28th February]. Temporarily they moved to Jane's mother's house in Laurencekirk, where their marriage was to take place – much against her mother's wishes. Jane had sold her furniture (perhaps to the new owner of the grocery business) with the exception of a heavy mahogany chest of drawers, a curtain (tent) bed and two trunks which contained some personal effects, including two Derbyshire spar ornaments. Archibald Spark, a carter residing in King's Lane in Montrose, was commissioned to deliver these to William Stephen residing near the flour mill in Aberdeen, who would arrange for their onward carriage to Inverness, where they would *lie until called for*. John assisted Archibald to load them on to the cart.

Prior to their move to Laurencekirk, Jane introduced John to her cousin, Margaret, and her husband, Colin Munro, who lived in Mill Street, Montrose. [Margaret's mother and Jane's mother were sisters]. Neither Margaret nor Colin had previously met John but on that occasion they conversed for two hours about the shop John had *looked out for Jane in Inverness* and about the many different places with which he and Colin were acquainted, including Aberdeen, Banff, Moray, Inverness and Ross-shire. [There is no record of John having ever been in Banff or Moray, other than when passing through on his travels to and from Montrose. He may also have been there during 1828-1830 when his whereabouts are less certain.] Margaret initially formed a favourable opinion of John, describing him as a *rational discreet sort of person*. However, she later changed that opinion and expressed disapproval of the proposed marriage because *the man was no' like her ava [at all]*.

Surprisingly, it was not until Saturday 7 March that arrangements were made for the marriage banns to be read. At 7.30 pm, accompanied by James Valentine [a master tailor in Montrose, whom John had befriended and had commissioned to make his wedding outfit], John called on John Younger, the Session Clerk of Montrose parish church, to ask for banns to be read for the 1st, 2nd and 3rd times on the following day, Sunday 8 March. When questioned by the Session Clerk, John declared that he was a sawyer by trade and had lived in Montrose for several months. As this story was corroborated by James Valentine, the Session Clerk considered there to be nothing improper and agreed to the request. [Although it was the Church of Scotland's preferred practice to read marriage banns on three successive Sundays, it was possible (for a fee) to have all three readings performed on the same day.]

A certificate verifying that the banns had been read was issued to John and Jane after the Sunday service, which they had both attended. The Montrose old parish register of marriages[12] records the proclamation on 8 March 1835: *John Adams, sawyer, and Jean*

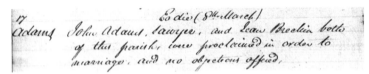

Figure 15: The marriage banns of John Adam and Jane Brechin in the Montrose old parish register of March 1835 (reproduced with permission of the Church of Scotland)

Brechin both of this parish, were proclaimed in order to marriage, and no objections offered. That evening John and Jane were invited to dinner by Jane's sister, Mary, and her husband, Archibald Gouk – the farmer on Rossie Island who had addressed the letters Jane had sent to John in Dingwall. Archibald had thought highly of John's conversation and considered him to be of *sound mind* – but Mary had expressed her displeasure with the proposed marriage due to the disparity in their ages.

Jane seems to have returned to Laurencekirk on the morning of Monday 9 March but John remained in Montrose to visit the two banks in which Jane had deposited money in April and June 1834. Showing remarkable trust in John's integrity, Jane had endorsed the backs of the original deposit receipts and had given them to John so that he could withdraw her savings before their marriage. At the British Linen Bank John was served by the on-duty teller, Robert Craigie, who requested him to countersign the back of the deposit receipt (no. 6/526) before paying him £97-16-8d, comprising the original £96 plus £1-16-8d interest. At the National Bank John was served by David Hill who asked if the endorsement on the back of the deposit receipt (no. 150) was in Jane's writing. On confirming that it was, John identified himself as John Adam employed as a 'sawyer in Montrose' and then countersigned the receipt. He was then handed £15-7/-, comprising the original £15 plus 335 days interest of 7/-. [By current banking standards, the ease with which John was able to withdraw the modern equivalent of almost £10,000 of Jane's money without any verification of his identity seems astonishing. When later asked to identify who had withdrawn the money, Robert Craigie could only recall John Adam being *a tall good looking man dressed in his Sunday clothes,* whilst David Hill *did not know to whom the money had been paid.*]

After his visits to the banks, John met with James Valentine to collect his wedding outfit – a blue coat with gilt buttons, a fancy vest with a red button at the top and snuff-coloured [later described as brown] trousers. They then went for a drink to celebrate the impending wedding. James Valentine later commented that John had a black pocket book with a considerable quantity of banknotes, which John had explained were back wages. One of the banknotes was described by James Valentine as 'bad' – being one issued by Maberly & Co.

[John Maberly was a successful entrepreneur who originally made his fortune supplying uniforms to the Army. In 1811 he purchased the Broadford linen works in Aberdeen, where he was given the freedom of the city and had the street in which his linen factory was situated named after him – Maberly Street. In 1818 he ventured into banking by founding his Exchange and Deposit Banks, based in Edinburgh. Although successful at first, the Banks had gone under by 1832 as a result of large unsecured overseas debts and a price war with the other Scottish banks. Because of the short existence of the Maberly Banks, their banknotes remain of particular interest to Scottish collectors.]

John returned to Laurencekirk during the afternoon of Monday 9 March and in the evening (accompanied by Jane's brother, Robert) went to see Rev John Cook, the parish minister of Laurencekirk. John produced the banns certificate from Montrose, dated Sunday 8 March, and Rev Cook agreed to perform the marriage ceremony on the following Wednesday. [John Cook, MA was the nephew of George Cook, who was the minister of Laurencekirk parish in 1795-1829 and was elected as Moderator of the Church of Scotland in 1825. He demitted his parish post in 1829 to become Professor of Moral Philosophy at St Andrews University. John Cook succeeded his uncle at Laurencekirk and served until 1845 when he moved to St Leonard's church in St Andrews. Both George and John were strenuous opponents of the Free Church of Scotland formed at the 'Disruption' of 1843.]

The wedding of John Adam and Jane Brechin took place on Wednesday 11 March 1835 at Jane's mother's house in Laurencekirk.

The marriage ceremony was conducted by Rev John Cook and among the witnesses were Jane's mother, sisters and brother. Archibald Gouk, Jane's brother-in-law, had also been invited but had arrived late. Notably, none of John's family attended – probably because none had been invited. The ceremony was scheduled for 12 noon but the bride had not been ready. Rev Cook entered into a long conversation with John whilst they waited. He was struck by John's *civility and apparent mildness of expression* and by his extensive acquaintance with the world and described him as having a very handsome countenance and figure. Conversely, he described Jane as *tho' not deformed, seemed less favoured in her visage by nature than almost any other woman* and surmised that the difference in their ages [46 vs 31] *highlighted the contrast*. Surprisingly, there is no record of the marriage in the Laurencekirk old parish registers[33]. Perhaps Rev Cook did not consider it necessary, as it was sufficient that the reading of the banns had been recorded in Montrose.

Immediately after their wedding ceremony, Mr and Mrs John and Jane Adam set off for Inverness. They initially took the Defiance stagecoach which left Laurencekirk at about 4.00 pm and reached Aberdeen via Stonehaven at about 7 pm[35]. They were still wearing their wedding clothes and their only luggage was a small 'reticule basket' [a pouch made of netted fabric used as a handbag] carried by Jane and a large open clothes basket carried by John – their other personal effects having previously been despatched on Archibald Spark's cart. On arriving in Aberdeen they would have sought a hotel or lodgings in which to spend the night. Next day they caught the 6.25 am Defiance coach out of Aberdeen to Inverness. It was a 4-horse coach calling at Huntly, Fochabers, Elgin, Forres and Nairn. The fare was £2 for inside passengers and £1-2/- outside.

The stagecoach arrived at the Caledonian Hotel in Inverness at 6.30 pm. John and Jane made their way to Fraser's public house to enquire about lodgings. They were directed to a house in Chapel Street where a vintner [wine merchant] named William Fraser and his wife, Catherine, lived. They were not able to offer a room but re-directed John and Jane next door to Hector and Janet MacIntosh,

Figure 16: An early-19th century Defiance stagecoach

who were able to provide accommodation. However, John had no plans to be with his wife that night. He stayed only to take some tea and then left, saying that he was going to Beauly by the North Mail coach which left Inverness every night at 9 pm bound for Thurso via Beauly, Dingwall, Tain and Dornoch. [Mail coaches were normally 'diligences' – a type of light coach introduced in about 1780 that carried three inside passengers. Some mail vans in the Highlands of Scotland still carry a limited number of passengers.]

Before leaving, John requested Hector MacIntosh to post two letters – one addressed to a John Beaton in the Haugh of Inverness, the other to James Noble, shoemaker, of Inverness. The content or purpose of these letters is not known, nor is any further reference made to them. They may have been letters of introduction, or letters given to John and Jane by relatives in Montrose for forwarding to acquaintances. [A 'haugh' is a flat area of alluvial meadowland beside a river. The Haugh of Inverness is on the east side of the Ness River just south of the castle. It is named as the 'Village of Haugh' on John Wood's 1821 town plan of Inverness[30].]

51

John did not catch the North Mail coach. Instead he took the Kessock ferry *en route* to Dorothy, his 'common-law' wife in Dingwall. [Although the term is often used, 'common-law' marriage never actually existed in Scotland. Irregular marriage by 'cohabitation and repute' applied to couples who lived together and were thought to be married.]

John shared the ferry crossing with two quarriers: Duncan Macdonald from the Bruichnain Quarry, Inverness; and Finlay Anderson from the Redcastle Quarry, on the Black Isle. Finlay took his leave soon after the ferry docked at North Kessock to walk west along the coast to Redcastle, whilst John and Duncan took the toll road which went north to join the 'parliamentary' road that traversed over the Mulbuie ridge from Conon Bridge to Fortrose. At the '½-way house' [Macdonald's Inn] on the top of the Mulbuie about a mile beyond the point at which the toll road joined the parliamentary road, they stopped for a drink. John ordered a glass of porter and Duncan a gill of whisky. John and Duncan then headed west along the parliamentary road to cross the Conon River at the new Conon Bridge [built in 1811 to replace the Scuddel ferry] before turning north along the shore of the Cromarty Firth to reach Dingwall.

Parliamentary roads and bridges[36] were built throughout the Highlands of Scotland in the late-18th and early-19th centuries to improve the economy of the area after the Jacobite rebellions. The only parliamentary road on the Black Isle was built in 1814-17 to connect the ferry at Chanonry Point (Fortrose) with the new Conon Bridge. The toll road to the Kessock ferry was a spur that branched off the parliamentary road at Cnoc an-acras, the old gaelic name [meaning the 'hungry hill'] for the area around the modern Tore roundabout. The Mulbuie (sometimes Mulbuy – but nowadays more commonly spelt 'Millbuie') is a ridge of high moorland that stretches along the spine of the Black Isle. It reaches a maximum height of 256 m at Mount Eagle.

John arrived home to be re-united with Dorothy around midnight. He was still carrying his 'bundle' and wearing his new coat, waistcoat and trousers, which he explained he had bought from his share of his father's legacy. He also informed Dorothy about the furniture that his aunt had left him and that a carter would soon be delivering it.

Next day (Friday 13 March 1835), using the name of Anderson, John deposited £100 (in £1 notes, 90 of which were British Linen Bank) with Ronald Gordon, teller at the National Bank in Dingwall. John also tried to collect the second letter that Jane had sent from Montrose in February – and that had been placed in the Dingwall post office window. However, the Postmaster, Roderick Hay, would not let him have it because it was addressed to John Adam. He subsequently sent it to the Dead Letter Office.

A week later, probably on Friday 20th March, on the pretext of being on business looking for some wood for his employer, John returned to the MacIntosh's house in Inverness to visit Jane. He explained to her that their house (which, on this occasion, he described as between Tarradale and Redcastle) was still occupied and would not be vacated for 2-3 weeks, so she would have to remain in Inverness for a little longer. After dinner John again departed for Dingwall.

During the weeks in which Jane was lodging in Inverness, she befriended Ann Anderson (neé Grant) who lived in one of the MacIntosh's upstairs rooms. On one occasion Ann accompanied Jane to purchase 1d worth of pills in Mackenzie's drug shop in Church Street and sometimes they went together to the River Ness to fetch water. Ann described Jane as a *quiet reserved woman who had no acquaintances in Inverness*. Ann's husband, James Anderson, who had also become acquainted with Jane, somewhat more bluntly described her as *a coarse-featured woman, marked with small pox*. Inevitably, Jane also became friendly with her landlady, Janet MacIntosh. She, too, was less than courteous in describing Jane as *stautish and plain, or ill-favoured*, whereas Jane's husband, John Adam, was considered *tall and good looking*. Janet MacIntosh had also remarked on the brevity of John's visits and his coldness towards Jane. Indeed, she had the impression that they did not seem to be on an affectionate footing.

Jane had developed acquaintances with other people too. For example, Ann Horack (neé Finister) of Academy Street, who came daily to Hector MacIntosh to buy bread, had frequently spoken to Jane. Mary Thomson (neé MacIntosh) of Academy Street was another. She had accompanied Jane to church on Sunday evenings.

Figure 17: Receipt for £100 deposited by John Adam in the Dingwall branch of the National Bank of Scotland in March 1835 (National Records of Scotland)

Across the Black Isle, the couple known as John and Dorothy Anderson had become well-respected in Dingwall. John Urquhart, their landlord, described John as *a sober man and good neighbour,* whilst his wife, Christian, had always found the couple to be *decent and quiet neighbours and very obliging.* However, Dorothy was again becoming unsettled. Although John had always been kind and attentive towards her, he had recently become aggressive at times and had also taken to sitting morosely at the fire for hours in silence, as though deep in contemplation, staring into the flames. Dorothy had made up her mind to leave him and go home to Derbyshire unless he married her. John had agreed that she could go in May and that he would follow her and marry her in England. She had been satisfied with that promise and had agreed to stay until then.

On Friday 27th March John returned again to the MacIntosh house in Inverness. He had crossed the Kessock ferry with Alexander Macleay and Thomas Ross, both from Dingwall. They had conversed about John's work in the Craig quarry. During the previous week, Jane had called into the carrier's office and had been informed that her furniture had arrived. From Aberdeen it had been taken to Elgin by William Stephen and then to Inverness by John Murdoch and his porter, a Chelsea Pensioner named Nicol Mackenzie. The charge was £2-6/- including storage in Inverness at 3d per day. On hearing the news, John immediately hired a horse and cart to convey the furniture to the Kessock ferry where, he said, it could be stored free in the tap room at Mackay's Inn at North Kessock until a carter could be commissioned to carry it to their house. During that afternoon Jane accompanied John to check that the furniture had arrived at the South Kessock pier. She then returned to her lodgings, requesting the MacIntoshs that she might stay until her husband had completed making her a comfortable room in their house, which she now described as being near the Scuddel ferry.

After Jane had left South Kessock, John took the furniture across the Kessock ferry and tried to have it carted over the Black Isle that evening. On the recommendation of Roderick MacGregor, one of the ferrymen, a local 'lad' was summoned to take the load to Conon Bridge. However, John was overheard telling the ferryman that he was going to Contin where the furniture would be collected and, on hearing this, the 'lad' (probably thinking he had been duped) refused to proceed. The ferryman then recommended Robert Thomson of Charleston (a little to the west of North Kessock) but it was too late to summon him and the furniture remained at Mackay's Inn where it was stored overnight. John probably also spent the night there because he had to ensure that none of the furniture, particularly the chest of drawers and the trunks, contained any of Jane's personal items. Dorothy would have been suspicious of anything that obviously did not belong to an elderly aunt, so John removed several such items and had them stored separately at Mackay's Inn to be collected later.

Next day, Saturday 28 March, John went to Charleston to ask Robert Thomson to convey the furniture from Mackay's Inn at North Kessock to Dingwall (with Jane's personal items removed, John could now specify that the load be taken direct to Dingwall, explaining that it had been bequeathed by a deceased female relative who had lived in the South). Robert Thomson agreed to take the load and went with John to Mackay's Inn, where the ferrymen assisted them to load his cart with what he described as *a bed, chest of drawers, trunk and deal box*. Accompanied by John, Robert took the load to the lodgings at John Urquhart's house in Dingwall. After unloading, John gave Robert a dram and paid him 5/-.

John's movements during the next week (Monday 30th March to Friday 3rd April) are not well recorded. He had work in the quarry but seems to have been ill for much of the week. On Monday 30 March, Dorothy had attended the funeral of a young girl, Helen Mackenzie, but John had not been there. However, John had recovered by the afternoon of Friday 3 April because he went to Inverness to see Jane and break the news that the house (near Scuddel Bridge) was now ready. After a dinner of barley broth and pork cooked by Jane, they packed up Jane's belongings and prepared to leave. Hector MacIntosh presented his bill for 3 weeks and 3 days lodgings – a small exaggeration as Jane had been there for exactly 21 nights, from Thursday 12 March to Friday 3 April. Nevertheless, Jane seems to have settled in full without dispute. Hector expressed surprise that they were leaving for Scuddel at such a late hour (5-6 pm, according to Hector) but John had said that they wouldn't go all the way that night – *perhaps 5 or 6 miles beyond the Kessock ferry, a bit further than Redcastle.* Janet MacIntosh noted that Jane was dressed in the same clothes as she had been wearing when she had arrived on Thursday 12 March – a black velvet bonnet, black veil, bluish-purple mantle and winchey [cotton flannelette] gown, crimson merino shawl [which Jane had bought for 4/6d] and a check verona [cotton and wool woven serge] handkerchief – also a light blue petticoat made by her mother. Jane also carried an umbrella and two baskets, one containing clothes and the other three pairs of stockings she had knitted for John during her stay in Inverness (one of which had not yet been finished). Ann Anderson also saw them leave, describing Jane as being *in high spirits to be going to her own house.*

The sun was already setting when Roderick MacGregor, the ferryman at Kessock ferry, set sail from South Kessock at 7 pm on Friday 3 April 1835. His only passengers were John and Jane Adam. On reaching North Kessock, they were last seen setting off into the gloaming on the toll road heading towards the Mulbuie.

Figure 18: The Kessock ferry in the 19th century

CHAPTER FIVE

Murder

A week later, on Friday 10 April 1835, Elizabeth (Betty) Gray and Margaret (Peggy) Stewart were working in Muillans Wood – a new plantation belonging to Sir Colin Mackenzie Bt, laird of the Kilcoy estate in the parish of Killearnan on the Black Isle. [Killearnan, which was sometimes called Redcastle, is a small parish lying in the south-west corner of the Black Isle. In the early-19th century its entire land area was owned by only three estates: Redcastle; Kilcoy; and Allangrange.]

Betty Gray and Peggy Stewart were half-sisters, having the same mother but different fathers. Both were unmarried and lived in Drumnamarg (now known as Croftcrunie), a farm in Cnoc an-acras (now known as Tore). They had been employed by Colin Young, ground officer [estate manager] of the Kilcoy estate, to replace small fir trees that had been frost-damaged over the winter. The wood lay (as it still does) on the southern slopes of the Mulbuie between two of Killearnan's crofting areas known as Heights of Kilcoy and Muckernich.

Originally, the Mulbuie was a 'commonty' – land in common ownership on which farmers and crofters could graze their animals in the summer, gather heather for roof thatching and cut peat for winter fuel. Around 1816, the heritors of the parishes of the Black Isle decided to divide up the Mulbuie amongst themselves according to the sizes of their estates. Much of the land was then planted with trees. The Kilcoy estate was allocated the land that, in 1833-34 when it was first planted, became Muillans Wood – so called because it was originally a moorland area where water from the wettest part of the Mulbuie, known as the Monadh Mor, was channelled into lade systems that provided water to drive the waterwheels of the estate corn mills – hence Muillins (or Millers) Wood.

Betty and Peggy had brought with them two children to help with the planting: Jane Stewart (age 13, daughter of Alexander Stewart of

Figure 19: Typical landscape of the Monadh Mor, the wettest area of the Mulbuie

Muckernich); and John Campbell (age 11, son of Donald Campbell of Drumnamarg). At around 8 am that morning, the children went to shelter from the cold April wind in the ruins of an old cottage – one of two that were located about 300 yards north of the ½ -way house [Macdonald's Inn] on the parliamentary road. Jane found a brown [later described as 'green kid'] glove lying on the ground and then noticed a piece of black gauze in a heap of stones and earth piled up in the corner of the ruins. Thinking that it might make a veil for her doll, she pulled on it but it would not come free, so she called Betty and Peggy. They, too, were unable release the gauze but spotted part of a shoe protruding from the other end of the heap and thought that there must be something buried there. On dislodging some of the stones and earth, they discovered that there was a foot in the shoe. Unwilling to disturb the heap any more, they sent the children to fetch William Forbes, who lived in 'End of Muckernich' about a quarter of a mile away.

Sixty year-old William Forbes was sitting at his fire when two children, whom he did not know, came to his house and explained that they had found some clothes at the old cottages. At first he did not respond to their pleas to go there but eventually the children persuaded him. When he arrived at the old cottage, he found that the walls and gables were generally around 4 ft high but that the south wall had been *thrown down* to form the heap. Using a spade, he cleared the stones and earth from around the shoe to expose a leg in a grey stocking. At the other end of the heap, he was *much shocked* to uncover a blood-stained face. He quickly re-covered the exposed body parts and went to find Alexander Macdonald, the 'changekeeper' [innkeeper] of the '½-way house'.

Figure 20: Macdonald's Inn (the ½ way house) on the Mulbuie ridge

On hearing William Forbes' exclamation that *it's a melancholy thing that's doon yonder [down there]*, Alexander Macdonald made haste to the ruined cottage, where he re-uncovered the leg and face. He immediately despatched John Campbell to Kilcoy Castle to find Colin Young, the ground officer. He also suggested that William Forbes go back to Muckernich to find Jane Stewart's father, Alexander, an elder of the church, desiring him to inform Rev John Kennedy, the Killearnan parish minister, and send for the Procurator-Fiscal in Dingwall. An hour later, Alexander Macdonald saw Sir Colin Mackenzie of Kilcoy passing along the parliamentary road in his carriage on his way to Dingwall. He ran out to inform the laird of the discovery of the body and was assured that Sir Colin would *carry intelligence of it to Dingwall.*

[In Scotland the 'Procurator-Fiscal' is the appointed law-agent of a burgh or shire, who institutes civil and criminal proceedings in the courts and prosecutes all criminal cases in the sheriff courts. In 1835 the Procurator-Fiscal of Dingwall was the 33-year old Hugh

Innes Cameron. He had also been elected as the town's Provost in 1833 and, with the exception of 1841, would retain this position until 1847. By profession he was a banker who became a Director of the Royal British Bank and was one of the eight Directors tried at the Court of the Queen's Bench in 1858 for conspiracy to defraud the Bank's customers in 1855 prior to its collapse in 1856. He was found guilty and given a 12-month custodial sentence.]

It was around 10 am when Colin Young arrived at the ruined cottage. Five women and Duncan Mackenzie, a carter from Dingwall, were there. Duncan had left home at 5 am to collect eggs from farms in the area for an egg merchant in Invergordon. He had travelled by Tarradale [near Muir of Ord], where he had learned that a body had been found, and had been on his way back home via the parliamentary road when he had enquired at the '½-way house' where the body was located. On arriving at the ruin, he had found the body covered by a pile of stones, earth and divots in the corner. To see if he could recognise it, he asked where the face was – and had already uncovered it by removing some earth and a *blooded stone* when Colin Young arrived.

Figure 21: A portrait of Hugh Innes Cameron, Procurator-Fiscal of Ross & Cromarty and Provost of Dingwall (reproduced with permission of Dingwall Museum)

Together, they removed some further stones and earth and revealed a black bonnet and veil – the very gauze to which Jane Stewart had been attracted two hours previously. Not recognising the body, Duncan Mackenzie then departed having been at the site for only ten minutes.

Before long, word of the body had circulated around the area and a considerable crowd had gathered in the old ruin. They included Donald Macdonald, a crofter in Muckernich, Hugh Mackay, the headmaster of the parish school, and Alexander and Kenneth Kennedy, two of the Rev John Kennedy's sons. No-one had dared to touch the corpse until James Macdonald of Muckernich arrived, having been informed of the body by the wife of Roderick Morrison. He described the scene as *like a market* and set about removing more of the stones and earth, hoping to discover the identity of the body. He uncovered the other leg, found the other green kid glove on the right hand of the corpse and noted a gold wedding ring on the third finger of the left hand. He also unearthed a shift [chemise or petticoat], the breast of which was embroidered with the initials 'IB' in red thread. He then put his hand into the deceased's 'pocket' [the reticule handbag] and pulled out four pence and a pill box containing two pills. Realising that the dead woman's identity was unlikely to be revealed by any further excavation, it was then decided to re-cover the body with some of the stones *lest dogs should get at it* and await the arrival of the Procurator-Fiscal.

Hugh Mackay had left his school earlier that morning to attend a meeting at the church. When he arrived there, he received a message to go to the manse to see Rev John Kennedy. The minister gave him a letter addressed to the Procurator-Fiscal with regard to the dead body. It was to be taken in haste to Dingwall by one of the pupils. Having despatched the pupil, Hugh and the minister's sons had progressed to the ruin to await the arrival of the Procurator-Fiscal. Two other people who arrived at the scene at that time were Catherine (known as Kate) Macdonald, the wife of the '½-way house' innkeeper Alexander MacDonald, and Alexander Noble, a retired Lieutenant in the East Middlesex Regiment who resided in Newton of Redcastle. Alexander Noble had been informed of the body by a man passing his house on his way to the meeting at the church.

At 1.30 pm one of the Ross & Cromarty Sheriff's officers arrived from Dingwall, accompanied by the pupil who had been sent from the school with the letter for the Procurator-Fiscal. He had intercepted the pupil en route as Sir Colin Mackenzie of Kilcoy had already informed the Procurator-Fiscal. The officer removed all the earth, stones and turf that had been replaced, hence fully exposing the body.

It was after 3 pm when the Procurator-Fiscal, Hugh Innes Cameron, arrived at the scene, accompanied by Sir Colin Mackenzie of Kilcoy and two doctors, Drs John Jones and William Hall. After examining the body he searched the ruin and the surrounding area for blood stains, footmarks or other evidence but could find none (although there must have been plenty of footprints – the area having been well trampled by the numbers of people who had come to see the body).

Leaving the doctors to make a detailed examination of the body, the Procurator-Fiscal soon turned his attention to questioning the witnesses and taking initial statements. Colin Young confirmed that three large stones, which appeared to have originated from the south wall of the ruin, had been removed from the body: one from the victim's face; one from the right breast; and one from the abdomen. Alexander Macdonald explained how he had been informed of the body that morning by William Forbes and revealed that he had passed the back of the ruin on the morning of Thursday 9 April but had not entered it and had not seen anything unusual. He also confirmed that he had not heard any cries or strange noises and had not seen anyone in the vicinity of the ruin the previous evening. William Forbes, who had temporarily left the scene to attend the meetng in the church, was interviewed on his return. He described how the two children had come to him around 8 am that morning, how he had sent for Alexander Macdonald, and how they had initially unearthed the leg and the face of the body before deciding to send for the Procurator-Fiscal.

Night had fallen before Hugh Cameron and the two doctors were satisfied that they had sufficient information on the location of the body and its mode of discovery. Clearly there had been a murder, but who was 'IB' with the gold wedding ring? No clue to her identity had been offered by any of the witnesses at the scene. At 7.00 pm, the removal of the body was authorised by the Procurator-Fiscal and, assisted by James Macdonald and Hugh Mackay, it was lifted onto a cart. During the removal two detached teeth were discovered, one lodged in the back of the corpse's neck. In the gathering darkness they set off for Dingwall and, later that evening, the corpse was laid out in the Town House.

Remarkably, that evening the *Inverness Journal*[37] of Friday 10 April 1835 published a letter describing the discovery of the body. It is prefixed by the statement: *The highly respectable writer of the following communication has given us his name and authorised us to refer to him.* The letter itself reads: *I think it my duty to communicate to you a piece of very melancholy information which I received a few hours ago, as I was passing over the Mulbuie for this place [Inverness]. This morning, as some men were employed in planting trees, near the summit of that dreary hill, they discovered the body of a young female, buried within the ruins of an old house there, with some large stones laid over the body. There seems no reason to doubt that this person met with a violent death, and she seems to have been of respectable connections, as a veil and bonnet were found upon the body. I afterwards met Kilcoy, on whose property the planting was carried on, travelling towards the spot, very probably with the view of instituting an enquiry into the circumstances of this distressing case; and as this is your publishing day, I think that no time should be lost in making the fact known to some who must feel a deep interest in the event. I am, &c. Viator.*

St Viator was a catechist of children at Lyons cathedral in the 4th century, suggesting that the source of the letter was a minister or teacher. Hence the probable writer was Hugh Mackay, the Killearnan parish school headmaster who was also a licensed preacher. He is recorded as having been at the site of the discovery in the morning but seems not to have returned until the evening, giving him plenty time to have visited Inverness. He probably wished to use a pseudonym to conceal his absence from school.

Back in Dingwall, one of Hugh Cameron's immediate tasks was to draw up a petition[38] addressed to John Jardine, the Sheriff of Ross & Cromarty, requesting permission for formal witness statements to be taken and for Drs Jones and Hall to examine the body. It reads:

That there was this day found on the site of an old house in a new plantation on the Heights of Kilcoy at a point between two hundred and three hundred yards from the High Road leading across the Millbuie in the parish of Killearnan and the County of Ross, the dead body of a female under such circumstances as to have no doubt she was cruelly murdered. May it therefore please your Lordship to grant warrant to Messrs Jones and Hall, Surgeons in Dingwall, with proper assistants to examine the body of the deceased in order the more certainly to discover the cause of her death, and to report thereon to your Lordship and also to grant warrant for the citation of such witnesses as the Petitioner may think proper to adduce to be examined in precognition in relation to the premises. According to Justice, (signed) H I Cameron, Procurator-Fiscal.

A response from Alexander Mackenzie, the Sheriff-Substitute of Ross & Cromarty, was received that evening: *The Sheriff-Substitute having considered the foregoing petition grants warrant to Messrs Jones and Hall, Surgeons in Dingwall, for the purposes set forth in the foregoing petition and also for the citation of witnesses to be examined as in precognition, all as prayed for. (Signed) A Mackenzie.*

Hugh Cameron also commenced the process of identifying the corpse by preparing a 'murder handbill' containing a full description of the body, the clothing, the wedding ring and the place of discovery[39]. Next day (Saturday 11 April) copies of the handbill were printed by Robert Carruthers of Inverness. [Robert Carruthers was the editor, sole proprietor and printer of the *Inverness Courier.*] Remarkably, these handbills had been hand-pressed and distributed locally throughout Easter Ross, the Black Isle and the Inverness area by Saturday evening and had been sent to all law enforcement agencies throughout Scotland by means of the Mail coach network.

After arranging for the wide distribution of the handbills, Hugh Cameron wasted no time in pursuing the only substantive lead that had emerged from his examination of the body – the pill box, which he noted was inscribed 'J. Mackenzie, Chemist and Druggist, Forres' (with the word 'Forres', a small town to the east of Inverness, scored out). He soon discovered that J. Mackenzie also had a shop in Inverness, so

MURDER!

WHEREAS the Body of a FEMALE was found about 8 o'clock in the morning of yesterday—FRIDAY—the 10th instant, in the ruins of a Hut within the new Plantation on the heights of Kilcoy, bearing such marks of violence as leave no doubt she was cruelly murdered.

APPEARANCE OF THE BODY.

The BODY is apparently that of a married woman about forty years of age; 5 feet 7 inches high, stout in figure; dark brown hair, mixed with some grey hairs, long at the back of the head, cut short over the forehead; wore a false front or curls of dark brown hair; coarse flat features, thick lips, small nose, marked by small pox; had a scar from the centre of the forehead downwards across the nose, and left cheek, 4½ inches in length, apparently occasioned by small pox, or a burn.

DRESS.

The DRESS was a black silk velvet bonnet, lined with black silk persian, trimmed with black silk ribbons; a net cap; a black figured bobbin net vail; a mantle of claret coloured cloth, bound with black satin; a check verona handkerchief; a small crimson merino shawl with a light border; a purple or puce worsted gown, (lindsey woolsey or winchey of home manufacture,) trimmed with velvet; a puce figured silk band; a light blue petticoat, and an under dark blue petticoat, both home made woollen stuff, a pair of coarse blue worsted stockings, white in the toes; cloth selvage garters; shoes such as usually sold in Shops, mended under the toes and heels: a cotton shift, marked on the breast with the letters I. B.; a coarse flannel jacket; a pair of drab jean stays; a pocket made of printed cotton, tied with a piece of blue striped tape, and containing four-pence of copper, and small pill box marked " J. Mackenzie, Chemist and Druggist, Forres," the last word scored through, wore a plain marriage ring marked " Gold," on the inside, on the 3d finger of the left hand; and gloves of green kid.

PLACE WHERE FOUND.

The PLACE where the body was found, is at the top of the Millbuie on the heights of Kilcoy, in the Parish of Killiernan or Redcastle, County of Ross, and between 200 and 300 yards in a straight line eastwards from the House of Alexander Macdonald, Changekeeper, which stands close to the Parliamentary Road leading over the Millbuie.

The Public are earnestly requested to communicate to the Procurator Fiscal of Ross, Dingwall, any circumstances which may lead to the discovery of the name and usual residence of the deceased, and of the person or persons by whom she has been murdered.

The body lies in the Town House of Dingwall, and will be kept uninterred, until Wednesday the 15th instant: to afford an opportunity of identifying it.

DINGWALL, 11th April, 1835.

Inverness: Printed by R. Carruthers.

Figure 22: The murder handbill issued by Procurator-Fiscal Hugh Cameron in April 1835 (National Records of Scotland)

a Sheriff's officer, Neil Duncan, was sent to investigate. The chemist, John Mackenzie, immediately recognised the box, which had contained 1d worth of rhubarb pills, two of which remained. However, neither he nor his assistants (Stephen Booth and Donald Paterson) could be sure to whom the pills had been dispensed, so Neil Duncan requested them all to accompany him to Dingwall to view the body. Neither of the assistants recognised the body but John Mackenzie thought that it *strongly resembled that of a female whom he had frequently served in the shop and who he thought was a resident of Inverness.* However, his recollection was that she had appeared to be *not a steady or respectable woman, unlike the body which was well dressed.*

Whilst Neil Duncan, the Sheriff's officer, was investigating the pill box, Procurator-Fiscal Hugh Cameron re-visited the Heights of Kilcoy. First he took a formal declaration (statement) from the 13 year-old Jane Stewart on how the corpse had been found and who had first removed earth and stones to reveal the body parts. Then, accompanied by Alexander Stewart, Jane's father, he went to interview Alexander Mackenzie, the innkeeper at the '½-way house' and his wife, Catherine (Kate). Both re-iterated in their formal declarations that they had never seen the deceased person before and had heard no screams or noises. However, Hugh Cameron seems to have harboured a theory that the murdered person, a stranger to the area, was likely to have visited the Inn. So he undertook a search the premises – but failed to find any evidence to support his suspicions.

The haste with which the murder handbills had been prepared on Saturday 11 April had been deliberate – and the pay-off was immediate. Knowing that a high proportion of the population respected the Sabbath, copies had been distributed to all the churches in time for the Sunday services on 12 April. Members of the congregation of the East Chapel (as it was then named) in Inverness were quick to respond when their minister, Rev Finlay Cook, read out the handbill. They included Hector MacIntosh and James Anderson of Chapel Street, who obtained a copy and showed it to their wives, who agreed that the description seemed to match that of the MacIntosh's ex-lodger, Mrs Jane Adam.

That Sunday afternoon the MacIntoshs and the Andersons contacted John Macbean, Messenger at Arms in Inverness, to alert him of their suspicions. [The 'Messenger at Arms' was the Burgh law officer responsible for serving documents, enforcing court orders and executing civil and criminal processes.] They were promptly conveyed to Dingwall to view the body which, despite its disfigurement, they immediately identified as Jane Adam and pointed out that one of the distinguishing features by which they could be sure of its identity was a missing front tooth, a detail that had not been mentioned in the handbill. They also recognised her clothing – including the shift with the embroidered initials 'IB' which were, in fact, 'JB'. They explained that Jane's maiden name was Brechin and that she had lodged with the MacIntoshs in Inverness whilst awaiting a house near Scuddel to be made ready by her husband, John Adam. The four witnesses provided a description of John and were taken to an Inn in Dingwall where they stayed the night.

The Sheriff's officers in Dingwall recognised the description given by Hector and Janet MacIntosh and James and Ann Anderson as a man who lived in Dingwall with another 'wife' under the name of Mr and Mrs Anderson. Very late that night (or very early the next morning – depending on the source of information) the officers, accompanied by John Macbean, went to the house at the west end of Main Street. They found John and Dorothy in bed. John was immediately handcuffed and taken to Dingwall Tolbooth, while the house was searched. A number of articles of female underclothing embroidered with 'JB' initials were found and £74 in banknotes was discovered in a black pocketbook under John's pillow.

Accompanied by the Procurator-Fiscal, John Adam was taken to view the corpse during the early morning of Monday 13 April. He denied having ever seen the deceased woman before and refuted that she had been his wife, asserting that his name was John Anderson, not John Adam, and that his wife was Dorothy Anderson who lived with him in Dingwall.

A remarkable conversation then took place. Although there is general unanimity, there are some variations in the exact words recorded in the several reports of it. The following is the version published in the *Inverness Journal* on Friday 17 April 1835.

Procurator-Fiscal: *Anderson, put your hand in that of the unfortunate woman and say was it ever there before?*
Prisoner: *No, it was not; I am not accustomed to see such awful sights.*
Procurator-Fiscal: *Anderson, put your hand on that bosom and say, before these persons, and your God, did your head ever rest on it?*
Prisoner: *No, it did not.*
Procurator-Fiscal: *Prisoner, touch those faded lips, and say did your's ever meet them in a kind embrace?*
Prisoner: (After considerable emotion, during which large drops of sweat were falling down the forehead): *No, no!*
Other reports then record that the Procurator-Fiscal concluded the conversation with the words: *Very well, we are all in the presence of God, who knows best.*

This process – in which a suspect is required to touch a murder victim – is variously called 'ordeal by touch', 'ordeal of the bier' or 'bier-right'. [A bier is the table, nowadays generally a trolley, on which a corpse is laid out.] In the medieval period, the wounds of a murdered corpse were supposed to bleed if the perpetrator touched them. There are many literary references to the ordeal (for example in Shakespeare's *Richard III*, Sir Walter Scott's *The Fair Maid of Perth* and Wagner's *Ring des Nibelunge*) but by the 18th century it had become a 'folk test' in which the behaviour of the suspect, when asked to touch the corpse, was recorded and could be given in evidence at a trial. There are a few instances of bier-right recorded in England and the USA in the 19th and early-20th centuries, but John Adam probably holds the distinction of being the last person in Scotland to be judicially put to the ordeal.

Following John's bier-right, the four witnesses from Inverness were brought to the Town House. They instantly recognised John Adam as the man whose wife had lodged with them. Two other witnesses from Inverness also arrived in Dingwall that morning to view the corpse: Ann Horack (neé Finister) – who had bought bread from the MacIntoshs

Figure 23: 'Ordeal of the Bier' scene from Wagner's *Ring des Nibelunge* in which the body of Prince Seigfried bleeds afresh as Princess Kriemhild accuses Hagan of his murder

every morning and had often spoken with Jane; and Mary Thomson (neé MacIntosh) – who had attended church with Jane on Sunday evenings. Both identified the body and recognised items of clothing, although Mary Thomson's later declaration indicated that she had doubts.

John persisted in his denial of any knowledge of the deceased woman but the Procurator-Fiscal was convinced that he was lying and immediately prepared a further petition to the Sheriff of Ross & Cromarty, this time for permission to arrest John[40]. It reads: *That in consequence of an information received by the Petitioner in course of last night and this morning in relation to the dead body of a female found on the Heights of Kilcoy in the parish of Killearanan and County of Ross – the Petitioner has reason to entertain strong suspicions that John Adam, alias Anderson, presently residing in Dingwall is guilty, actor [alone] or art and part [accessory], of the death of the said female. May it therefore please your Lordship to grant warrant to Officers of Court with legal concurrents to apprehend the said John Adam, alias Anderson, and to bring him before your Lordship for examination. According to Justice, (signed) H I Cameron, Procurator-Fiscal of Court.*

A response was received from Alexander Mackenzie, the Sheriff-Substitute, later that same day: *The Sheriff-Substitute having considered the foregoing petition, grants warrant to Officers of Court with legal concurrents to apprehend John Adam, alias Anderson, complained of and to bring him before the Sheriff for examination. (Signed) A Mackenzie.* John was duly formally arrested and members of the Ross-shire militia were assigned to guard him in the Dingwall Tolbooth overnight.

Next day, Tuesday 14 April, Procurator-Fiscal Hugh Cameron, convinced that he needed John Adam to be properly jailed (rather than detained under guard), petitioned the Sheriff of Ross & Cromarty for permission to commit John Adam to prison in Inverness[41]. The petition reads: *That John Anderson or Adam, apprehended on the morning of the 13th inst on suspicion of having been guilty, actor or art and part, of the murder of the female whose dead body was found in the ruins of a hut in a new plantation on the heights of Kilcoy, in the parish of Killiernan and County of Ross, on the morning of the 10th inst, and which body has been since identified as that of Jane Brechin, sometime resident in Montrose, and recently married to the said John Anderson, or Adam – having been twice judicially examined in the presence of his Lordship the Sheriff-Substitute, and a certain progress having been made in the precognition anent [about] the murder of the said female, and it being now apparent that the suspicion on which the said John Anderson, or Adam, was apprehended, was well founded, and that he is guilty, actor or art and part, of the murder of the said female, the present application is made praying: That your Lordship, in consideration of the premisses grant warrant for committing the said John Anderson, or Adam, to prison, therein to remain until he be liberated in due course of law; and, in respect, that the gaols of this Sheriffdom are insecure and unfit for the safe custody of the said John Anderson, or Adam, to grant warrant for his removal to the Tolbooth of Inverness, and for his incarceration within, requesting the concurrence of the Sheriff of Inverness and the Magistrates [the title given to a Provost or Bailie of a burgh by virtue of conferred powers of criminal and civil jurisdiction] thereof, in the incarceration of the said John Anderson, or Adam, in the said Tolbooth until he be therefrom liberated in due course of law. According to Justice, (signed) H I Cameron, Procurator Fiscal.*

The jails of Ross & Cromarty in the early 19th century were in a poor state. In 1829 a report[42] issued by the Justices of the Peace of Ross-shire described the Tolbooth in Dingwall [which was located in the Law Courts, now the Town Hall] as in *so extremely bad a state in all the respects required by the statute as to be utterly useless and even unfit for the habitation of human beings.* The report concluded that *it is necessary to erect a new gaol and court house in the Burgh – and that as the funds of the Burgh are inadequate to repay more than a small proportion of the expense, the Magistrates should grant a sufficient extent of land on which to erect the building and give the materials of the present building, and that the further cost of the same should be defrayed by the Burgh and the County in the proportion of one-fourth from the former and three-fourths from the latter.* The consequence of the report was that in 1830 the Tolbooth was declared unfit to receive prisoners and a new jail was never built. It had therefore become normal for the Burgh of Dingwall to send its prisoners awaiting their trials to be detained in Tain Tolbooth, which had been renovated in 1825. However, this created difficulties for the Magistrates of Dingwall – as explained in the Burgh minutes[43] of 4 June 1835 which record that: *not only was the want of a jail in Dingwall a great evil as occasioning the imprisonment in Tain of a greater number of delinquents than the jail should contain and thereby subjecting the prisoners to what was equivalent to additional punishment, but the expense actually occurred in the transmission of prisoners amounted to a larger sum than it would cost to repair the jail in Dingwall, so as to make it sufficient as a place of temporary confinement.*

As stated above, the practice of sending Dingwall's prisoners to Tain jail created serious overcrowding, so the Magistrates of Tain petitioned the Lords Commissioners of Justiciary in Edinburgh that the practice should stop. The response, copied into the minutes of the Burgh of Dingwall, was that: *the Magistrates of the Burgh (of Tain) are no longer bound to receive any criminal prisoners into their jail sent from any of the districts of Dingwall, Fortrose or*

Cromarty, as also, in the event of its being or becoming necessary from the want of due accommodation in the said jail of Tain. So that Ross & Cromarty's prisoners could be accommodated, supposedly until repairs were undertaken at the Dingwall Tolbooth, the Lord Commissioners declared that Inverness jail and all forts (in particular Fort George) could be temporarily used as 'legal prisons'. It was under the provisions of this declaration that it was possible for John Adam to be detained in Inverness, as long as the Magistrates of Inverness agreed. [Repairs to the Dingwall Tolbooth in October 1835 are recorded in the Burgh minutes but it was never again authorised as a 'legal prison'.]

Figure 24: Dingwall Town House and Tolbooth in the early-19th century
(© Crown Copyright: RCAHMS. Licensor www.rcahms.gov.uk)

CHAPTER SIX

Precognition

Whilst an answer to his petition to transfer John Adam to Inverness was awaited, Procurator-Fiscal Hugh Cameron continued to elicit the help of the Ross-shire Militia in securing John in the Tolbooth at Dingwall. Then, in the presence of Alexander Mackenzie, Sheriff-Substitute of Ross & Cromarty, he conducted a judicial examination and interrogation of John, thus commencing the process of 'precognition' – the practice in Scots law of taking preliminary statements (or declarations) from witnesses to determine if there are grounds to mount a prosecution[44]. What John provided in his 52-page declaration of 14 April 1835 was an extraordinary mixture of semi-truth and outright invention. The following summarises the main points:

That his name is truly John Anderson and was never known by any other name ... that he was born close to Dalkeith ... that his father was James Anderson, who died 5 or 6 years ago, and was a farmer on the Duke of Buccleugh's estate at Townhead ... that he attended, during the winter months only, the schools of Mr Mackay and Mr Louden in Dalkeith for 3 and 2 years respectively ... that he learned reading, writing and arithmetic with book-keeping ... that he left at the age of 18 [sic] years and worked for a few years with his father on his farm ... that in 1827 or 1828 he left to enter service at Mr Haig's distillery at Lochrin as a maltster ... that he stayed for 2 years before entering service in 1829 or 1830 until 1831 or 1832 as a ploughman of Mr Crichton, the tenant of Newbarns farm, 3 miles east of Cupar Angus ... that Mr Crichton took a lease of Barnhill farm, 3 miles from Nottingham ... that he worked there as an overseer at £40 per annum for 2 years and 9 months ... that he left in February 1834 when Mr Crichton became bankrupt and his stock was sold by his creditors ... that he was paid by Mr Crichton up to the term of Whitsunday [28

May] ... that Mr Crichton gave him a certificate of character which is in his lodgings in Dingwall ... that he returned by mail and stage coach to Townhead, where his mother still resides as a tenant of part of the farm which his father occupied.

That about the New Year of 1834 he married Dorothy Elliott, the daughter of Edward Elliott, a publican in Mansfield, a town about 8-10 miles from Barnhill ... that they were married by licence by Rev Alexander Fisher, Curate at Mansfield ... that the witnesses were Dorothy's sister, Elizabeth, and an acquaintance named John Gall ... that Dorothy remained with her parents while he worked at Barnhill ... that the certificate is in a small accounting book with a blue cover in the centre top drawer of the chest in their lodgings ... that they travelled north together in February 1834 and remained at Townhead for about 3 weeks to come to Inverness in the first week of April via Edinburgh, Aberdeen by Mail Coach, then Defiance to Inverness ... that they remained in Inverness, staying at 3 Gordon Place, to change two £5 notes of the Nottingham Bank ... that 10 days later he received a letter containing a £10 Bank of England note ... that they then travelled to Dingwall and took lodgings with John Urquhart, where they continue to reside.

That he came to Inverness because he had a letter of introduction from Mr Crichton to Mr MacIntosh of Raigmore but that he was told by his neighbour that he was a fashious [sic] person, so was dissuaded from going to him ... that he had burnt the letter as he had determined not to make use of it ... that he and Dorothy had come to Dingwall because he had been told by some acquaintances that he was more likely to obtain agricultural employment in Ross-shire ... that he had called at Major Mackenzie of Fodderty looking to be engaged on his farm but was disappointed ... that the next day he went to a farm of the Earl of Dingwall, occupied by John Munro ... that he could get work in trenching but the wages offered were too low ... that on returning to Dingwall he had passed by a quarry where he had observed his landlord, John Urquhart, at work ... that he had entered the quarry where the tenant, David Sutherland, had given him work starting the next day at 18d [1/6d] per day ... and that when the days were longer he was paid 20d [1/8d].

That when he came to Dingwall he had only the £10 that he had exchanged in Inverness ... that when he went to Townhead from Barnhill he had £55 and some shillings ... that he had lent £40 of that money to his brother, James ... that the balance of £15 had been spent on coach fares (4 guineas) and accommodation ... and that £10 had remained when they came to Dingwall.

That there was no work in the quarry for 2 months in the depth of winter and only occasional work within the last 2 or 3 weeks ... that sometime about the beginning of March he had visited Townhead ... that he had travelled the greater part of the way by foot ... that his purpose was in connection with a letter he had received from his brother, James, telling him that money left by an uncle who had died in Antigua was about to be paid and he was required to sign the papers ... that he had been told he was to inherit £180 but it had not arrived ... that he was informed that the money would not now be remitted until August, although it would then amount to considerably more than the amount first promised ... that he took up the £40 previously lent to his brother and got £70 from his mother as his share of his father's succession ... that all the money was paid in £1 notes of different banks ... that he remained at Townhead for 2 weeks but had not attended church so could not name the minister of the parish ... that he travelled back via Edinburgh where he stayed 3 days with his cousin, William Anderson, an apprentice with a hardware merchant, who lives at 38 Princes Street ... that he left Edinburgh on a Wednesday by Defiance stagecoach to Aberdeen ... that he continued to Inverness on the next day as an outside passenger arriving before 8pm ... that he does not know the names of the guards or the other passengers who were taken up or set down at Huntley, Keith, Forres and Campbelltown [Ardersier] ... that he went to Wilson's Hotel in Inverness and drank a porter until at 9 pm he heard the sound of the trumpet of the Mail starting for the North ... that he arrived in Dingwall that Thursday night.

That he was absent from Dingwall between 4 and 5 weeks from the day he set off until the day he returned ... that 3-4 days later he banked £100 with the National Bank in Dingwall and received receipt no. 7/141, in favour of Mr John Anderson, dated 13 March ... that he resumed work in the quarry but during the third week he was sick and for three days was confined to his bed.

That on the Saturday after he was ill he went to Inverness to collect furniture ... that he met two persons at Mackay's stables in North Kessock who had come from Dingwall on horseback ... that he thought they were clerks or writers ... that the furniture had been left to him by an aunt whose name was Janet Bunton ... that the furniture consisted of a mahogany chest of drawers, a bed, a small trunk and a small square deal box ... that the chest contained various articles of female apparel and bed and table linen and that the trunk contained sheets and articles of that sort ... that he has two sisters: Margaret who is married to William Anderson, a cousin who is a carter in Dalkeith; and Janet who is unmarried and lives with his mother at Townhead ... that he does not know why his aunt left clothes to him, rather than his sisters ... that the chest, trunks and bed lay in his mother's house at Townhead since his aunt's death ... that his aunt was about 40 years old and had made a will which was at his mother's house ... that the articles had been sent by his brother, James, by ship from Leith to Aberdeen, then to Inverness and to South Kessock where they had lain since the previous day ... that he had mislaid the receipt but the sum that he had paid was £2-6/- ... that he did not know the name of the carter ... that he took the articles across the ferry to the north side and there hired a porter named Thomson whom he accompanied to Dingwall, where they arrived about ten o'clock at night ... that these articles were the only ones left to him by his aunt except for a pretty large chest of bed clothes which remains at his mother's house at Townhead ... that whilst the chest of drawers was in the tap room at North Kessock awaiting the carter, he removed a shirt and stockings which he wanted to take to Dingwall in case the furniture could not be conveyed to Dingwall that day ... that he had replaced the shirt and stockings when he was assured that Mr Thomson would convey everything to Dingwall that night ... that he had carried the keys to the chest and the trunk in his pocket from Townhead ... that all the articles marked 'JB' were for Janet Bunton.

That on a previous visit from Dingwall to Inverness he had met with George Wilson, a blacksmith who originates from Dalkeith, on business ... that Wilson is employed by Mr Napier at a foundry near the Broomielaw in Glasgow ... that they had met in the Caledonian Inn near the Canal ... that Wilson was an old friend from Mr Mackay's school in Dalkeith ... that he met Wilson for about an hour and then went, as work at the quarry was not regular, to try to get work as a labourer at the public buildings being erected on the Castle Hill ... that he also visited the carter's premises to enquire about the furniture and was told by the carter's wife that it was expected on the next Friday ... that he had asked her to send the furniture to the Kessock ferry, where he would collect it on the Saturday.

That he had not since been in Inverness or the Ferry on any occasion whatever ... that during the next week he had been ill and though only confined to his bed for three days, had not felt himself stout enough to work at the quarry and that during the whole six days he did not go out of the house at all ... that he had attended church on the afternoon of Sunday 5 April ... that on 6, 7 and 8 April he worked in the quarry ... that on Thursday 9 April he went to the house of William Miller, changekeeper in Dingwall, to meet by appointment at two o'clock John Michael (or Macdonald) about hiring a horse for the season ... that Michael (or Macdonald) left between eight and nine o'clock by which time the deal had been concluded ... that the terms of the deal were 11 guineas for the season, £5 on account, and £20 as security that the horse would be returned ... that before he took possession of the horse on Friday 10 April, he drew the money from the bank at about twelve o'clock ... that he uplifted the whole £100 that he had previously deposited ... that he wanted some things for his house but did not know how much money he might need and could afterwards repay the balance into the bank ... that he took possession of the horse between two and three o'clock and went away to the country ... that he went south to Maryburgh and the Scuddle Bridge, then east through Ferintosh to Culbokie where he remained that night, but does not remember the name of the Innkeeper ... that he called at different farm houses requesting employment of the horse and got promises from various tenants ... that he does not remember the names of the farmers except one named Allan ... that on Saturday (11 April) he journeyed over the heights to the high road from Scuddle to Kessock ... that he joined this road at 5 or 6pm at a point where there is a house with a sign and where a tailor lives, then direct to the Scuddle bridge and home to Dingwall.

That on Sunday (12 April) his wife was very poorly and did not go to church ... that during the night between Sunday and Monday he was taken into custody by Mr Macbean ... that on the Saturday evening he had been told by his wife that the dead body of a woman had been found in an old house in a new plantation and nigh to a public house on the road between Scuddle and Kessock Ferry ... that he did not hear the circumstance mentioned until it was told to him by his wife ... that he had later heard the wife and daughter of his landlord talking of the circumstance ... that he had heard the next day that the female had been murdered and that the body had been brought to Dingwall ... that it grieved him much to find now that this was laid to his charge, and him innocent ... that with apprehension he was taken by the Procurator-Fiscal to see the body ... that he did accordingly lay his hand upon the face and bosom and take her hand in his ... that he never saw the body before that time, alive or dead ... that he had no hand in the death and exclaimed: 'may God forbid that he should, in her's or any other person's, and that he takes God to witness that he is innocent'.

That he was never in Montrose and does not know of the town of Alyth nor of the name of Craigieloof ... that he never was a soldier and never served in a cavalry regiment, and does not know of the town of Wirksworth in Derbyshire ... that he was never married to any woman except Dorothy Elliott ... that he had never before seen the elderly woman introduced to him by Mr Macbean or the elderly man introduced to him by the Fiscal ... that he never knew anyone in Inverness by the name of MacIntosh nor Anderson ... that he was never in any house in Chapel Street, Inverness ... that he was only ever in a house in Gordon Place in the spring of 1834, in the Coach and Horses Inn of John Macdonald, in the hotel kept by Mr Wilson where the Defiance Coach stopped, and in the house where the carrier from Aberdeen lives ... that he knows the public house near to the place where the body was found, having gone along that road several times ... and that he knows the situation of the plantation but does not recollect any ruins of a house in it.

The declaration is annotated: *The following declaration written upon this and the fifty one preceding pages, and freely and voluntarily emitted by the Declarant, who appears to be sober and of a sound mind, and the said being read over to him, he adhered thereto in all points before these three witnesses: Hugh Innes Cameron, Procurator-Fiscal of Court of Dingwall; Mr John Macbean, Messenger at Arms in Inverness; and Robert Falconer, Clerk to the said Hugh Innes Cameron, and Writer thereof.*

Figure 25: John Adam's signature as his assumed name of John Anderson (National Records of Scotland)

Although much of this statement is fantasy, John did hire a horse on Friday 10 April. He had visited the Bank on that day and had withdrawn the £100 that he had deposited on 13 March. The bank teller, Ronald Gordon, recalled that John was paid in £5 notes of the National Bank, plus 3/- interest. Robert Gordon had also been called to John and Dorothy's house on Monday 13 April when the Procurator-Fiscal and John Macbean had found the black leather pocket book. He had confirmed that it contained £74, comprising fourteen National Bank £5 notes and four £1 notes, one of which was a 20/-note of John Maberly & Co. He had also seen the receipt acknowledging the payment to John Macdonald of £20 security and £5 pre-payment for the hire of a horse for the season. Thereafter, Robert Gordon had attended the Town House to verify that the person in custody was the same John Anderson who had deposited and withdrawn the £100. In the Town House he had been a witness to the bier-right. It was also established, and later confirmed by Dorothy Elliott, that John was away from home on the night of Saturday 11 April. Whether he was trying to hire out the horse for spring ploughing as he claimed in his statement, or whether he had some other purpose, was never established.

Also that day, the Procurator-Fiscal received formal declarations from: John Campbell, Peggy Stewart and Betty Gray – who had discovered the corpse; William Forbes, Alexander Macdonald, James Macdonald and Duncan Mackenzie – who had partially unearthed the corpse to try and identify it; Colin Young, Alexander Noble, Catherine (Kate) Macdonald and Hugh Mackay – who had been witnesses to the various activities that had taken place after the discovery of the corpse at the murder scene; and Roderick MacGregor – who had ferried John and Jane Adam from South Kessock on the evening of Friday 3 April.

The remarkable speed with which the mail coaches were able to distribute the murder handbills throughout Scotland was well illustrated on Tuesday 14 April when a letter from Robert Burness, Procurator-Fiscal of Montrose, arrived at Hugh Cameron's office. It enclosed statements given to John Barclay, Provost of Montrose, by three witnesses who had read the description of the dead body in the handbill and had recognised it as that of Jane Brechin. The statements were from Margaret Munro (neé Garden), Jane's cousin, and her husband Colin Munro of Mill Street, Montrose; and Archibald Gouk, Jane's brother-in-law, who farmed at Rossie Island, Craig. They all confirmed the sale of Jane's shop, the despatch of her furniture to Inverness and the circumstances of her marriage to John Adam in Laurencekirk. Margaret Munro also pointed out that Jane had recently lost a front tooth and this distinguishing feature had been omitted from the description in the handbill.

After John Adam's declaration had been taken, a copy was immediately sent to the Sheriff of Ross & Cromarty. As permission to transfer John to Inverness jail was still awaited, the copy of the declaration was accompanied by a request that John should remain in custody in Dingwall. An acknowledgement was received from Alexander Mackenzie that same day (Tuesday 14 April): *The Sheriff-Substitute having again considered the foregoing petition and complaint, together with a judicial declaration this day emitted before him by John Adam(s), alias Anderson, complained of, with the declarations of sundry witnesses examined as in a precognition of the premises as far as hitherto led, and which declarations are taken down on paper apart, grants warrant to Officers of Court and their assistants to detain the said John Adam(s), alias Anderson, in custody for further examination. (Signed) A Mackenzie.* John was therefore detained for a second night, guarded by the Ross-shire militia in Dingwall Tolbooth.

Next day, Wednesday 15 April, two further letters from Robert Burness arrived at the Procurator-Fiscal's office in Dingwall. They contained four statements from: (i) James Beattie, the British Linen Bank's agent [manager] in Montrose – stating that Jane Brechin had deposited £96 on 3 June 1834 and had indorsed John Adam to uplift it on 9 March 1835; (ii) Robert Craigie, the teller at the British Linen Bank – confirming that he had paid out the sum of £97-16-8d to John Adam; (iii) Mary Gouk (neé Brechin), Jane's sister and wife of Archibald Gouk – describing Jane's employment with William Smart at Cairnbank, the opening of Jane's grocery shop in Castle Street at Whitsunday 1833, Jane's letters to John Adam addressed by her husband, and Jane's marriage on 11 March 1835 to John Adam at her mother's house in Laurencekirk; and (iv) Archibald Spark, the Montrose carrier – confirming that he had delivered Jane's furniture to William Stephen in Aberdeen for onward transmission to Inverness.

That same day, a statement was taken from Catherine Fraser (neé Fowler), wife of William Fraser, the vintner in Inverness. She had been brought to Dingwall by John Macbean, Messenger at Arms, and described how a well-dressed, tall couple had called at her house in Chapel Street one Sunday about a month ago, looking for lodgings [actually, they had arrived on Thursday 12 March – a confusion that was later to create doubt over the actual date of the murder]. She had directed them to Hector and Janet MacIntosh next door. Catherine was then requested to participate in an identity parade from which she readily identified John Adam, and to view the corpse which she thought *resembled the woman*.

The local press were now vigorously following every new

development and were vying to be the first to publish details as they emerged. Although it had been 'scooped' by the publication of Viator's letter on Friday 10 April in the *Inverness Journal*, the rival *Inverness Courier* was able on Wednesday 15 April to provide its readers with the first full report of the murder. Under the headline 'Suspected Murder of a Wife by her Husband', it relates the discovery of the corpse and all the subsequent events that had led to the identification of the victim and the arrest of John Anderson (Adam). In an otherwise very accurate report, it makes only one error – a mistaken statement that prior to their journey north, Jane Brechin was married to John Anderson (Adam) *some years since and deserted by him*. It concludes with a surmise that John *will be committed to Inverness jail this evening to await his trial before the Circuit Court of Justiciary in Autumn next.*

A day later than surmised by the *Inverness Courier*, two responses to Procurator-Fiscal Hugh Cameron's request for permission to commit John Adam to prison in Inverness[40] were received on Thursday 16 April. The first was from the Sheriff-Substitute of Ross & Cromarty, and reads: *The Sheriff-Substitute having considered the foregoing petition, and also the two petitions addressed to him by the Procurator-Fiscal, on the 10th and 13th instant, as also the judicial declarations emitted before the Sheriff upon the 14th instant, and of this date, by John Anderson or Adam complained of, together with the declarations of the witnesses already examined as in a Precognition of the premises – grant warrant to Mr John Macbean, Messenger at Arms, with legal concurrents, to convey the said John Anderson or Adam, prisoner, to the Tolbooth of Inverness; and the Sheriff-Substitute earnestly requests that the Sheriff of Inverness, or his Substitute, will concur in this warrant ordaining the said John Anderson or Adam, in respect of the circumstances stated in the foregoing petition, to be committed prisoner to the Tolbooth of Inverness, therein to remain until he be liberated in due course of law. (Signed) A Mackenzie.*

The second response was from the Sheriff-Substitute of Inverness and reads: *The Sheriff-Substitute of Inverness-shire in respect of the circumstances stated in the petition and the request of the Sheriff-*

Substitute of Ross made in his warrant issued thereon, concurs as desired, and grants warrant for committing the said John Anderson or Adam within the Tolbooth of Inverness therein to remain until liberated in due course of law. (Signed) J Edwards.

Having now obtained permission to transfer his prisoner to the Tolbooth in Inverness, Hugh Cameron asked John whether, in the light of the statements made by witnesses from Inverness and Montrose, he wanted to add anything or alter any part of the judicial declaration that he had made on Tuesday 14 April. John responded that he did not but would supplement his statement with some further information. This 2nd declaration, like his 1st declaration, was taken by Hugh Cameron in the presence of Alexander Mackenzie, Sheriff-Substitute of Ross & Cromarty. The following is a summary of the main points contained within the nine-page declaration:

That the Public House standing by the road side, nigh to the new plantation in which the dead body was said to be found, stands upon the right hand side of the high road as one goes to Kessock from Scuddle ... that it is about two miles nearer Kessock than the house with the sign where a tailor resides and where he joined the high road on the evening on Saturday 11th inst, when returning with his horse to Dingwall ... that on passing the tailor's house he spoke to a woman having the appearance of a servant girl whether her master was at home, and to which she answered that he was not ... that he spoke to no other person until he came to the village of Scuddle (or Cononbridge) when he spoke to Hector Mackenzie, Innkeeper there, requesting from him employment of his horse ... that until he reached his lodgings, he never heard from anyone, man or woman, that the dead body was found in the plantation ... that he had been in the Public House on the road going to Kessock when he and his wife were coming for the first time, last year, to Dingwall ... that they had stopped there for a quarter of an hour while they drank a bottle of porter once last year ... that, except on that occasion, he never was in that Public House.

That he does not know the 2nd Dragoons nor whether they are, or are not, sometimes called the 'Queen's' or 'Queen's Bays' ... that he does not know Colonel Hay nor, so far as he knows, did ever see a person of that name and rank ... that he was never in the town of Derby or remembers the assizes being held there in the spring of last year ... that he does not know of the village of Duffield ... that he never knew a person by the name of Archibald Gouk or Jane Brechin ... that he came through Laurencekirk when he was last south but does not know anybody residing there ... that he does not know Margaret Gordon, or Colin Munro or his wife, or Archibald Spark or Mary Brechin (or Gouk) ... that he never was on Rossie Island unless it was on the road that the coach travels ... that he does not know either the man or the woman brought this day by the Procurator-Fiscal into the room ... that he heard the woman pronounce the words 'it was you, John, took awa my cousin' but does not know what the woman meant.

As before, this second declaration was annotated: *The foregoing declaration written upon this and the eight preceding pages, by Robert Falconer, Clerk to Hugh Innes Cameron, Procurator-Fiscal of Court, Dingwall, was freely and voluntarily emitted by the Declarant, who appears to be sober and of a sound mind, and the same being read over to him, he adheres thereto in all points before these witnesses: the said Hugh Innes Cameron; John Inglis Nicol, Surgeon in Inverness; and the said Robert Falconer, writer hereof.*

That same day (Thursday 16 April) the initial report of John Jones and William Hall, the doctors assigned to examine the corpse, was received by the Procurator-Fiscal. Their report states: *We the undersigned, surgeons in Dingwall, having at the request of Hugh Innes Cameron, Procurator-Fiscal for the County of Ross, accompanied him on Friday 10th instant to the Heights of Kilcoy in the parish of Killearnan, we were there shewn the body of a female lying in an angular situation in the south east corner of the ruins of a hut within the new plantation on the Heights of Kilcoy, partly covered with turf, sand and stones, evidently a part of the wall of the hut. After minutely examining the position in which the body lay, and the surrounding objects, we found on raising the head a considerable quantity of cloated blood lying on the ground. No person of a crowd of people present could recognise the body and being unable to make the necessary examination of the body at this place, it was by order of the Fiscal removed to the Court House at Dingwall, where on examination we observed the following appearance:*

The body to be that of a stout muscular female, apparently 40 years of age or upwards. The face much swollen and of a bright livid appearance, the tongue thrust about an inch out of the mouth, and from the nose there was a discharge of blood. Under the right ear the skin was much discoloured and a deep indentation of the integuments, under which there was a fracture of the lower jaw bone, and a fracture of the same bone on the left side, near the angle of the mouth. On the head there were two lacerated wounds of the scalp, of a triangular shape and corresponding with the corner of a stone found under the head of the deceased. We could discover no other external marks of violence on the body. Upon dissection we found the vessels of the brain distended with dark coloured blood, but in no degree sufficient to explain the cause of death. The brain was firm and natural in every part. The right lung adhered universally but its structure was natural. The left lung was healthy. The heart was loaded with fat but presented no diseased appearance. The stomach contained a quantity of fluid like barley broth, and the contents of the abdomen were generally healthy.

From our examination and dissection of the body, we have no hesitation in stating it to be our opinion that death was caused by the violence of the blows the deceased sustained about the head. The Fiscal having ordered the body to be preserved in ceure [protective] cloth in order that it may be identified by persons who have to come from a distance, it still lies in the Court House for that purpose. Certified on soul and conscience this 16th day of April 1835 by John Jones and William Hall, Surgeons.

A report by John Inglis Nicol MD, who had been a witness to John Adam's 2nd declaration taken earlier that day, was also received on Thursday 16 April. It states: *I hereby certify on soul and conscience that (at) the request of Hugh I Cameron Esq, Procurator-Fiscal for the County of Ross, I this day examined the body of a woman lying in the Court House of Dingwall, and am of the opinion that the individual must have been dead from twelve to fifteen days.*

The local press was maintaining its lively interest in every detail of the story as it unravelled. Following up Viator's letter on the previous Friday, the *Inverness Journal* of Friday 17 April described for its readers: the examination of the corpse at the murder scene by the Procurator-Fiscal and the two doctors; the identification of the corpse by the two witnesses brought to Dingwall by John Macbean; the bier-right to which John Adam had been subjected; and the witnesses' subsequent identification of him. It also revealed that one of its reporters had visited John in the Inverness Tolbooth that morning and that he had denied the murder – claiming that *it would hurt the feelings of his friends to hear that he stood accused of such a crime.*

Not surprisingly, in the light of the Forfarshire roots of both the murder victim and the accused, the *Montrose, Arbroath and Brechin Review* also carried a full article on Friday 17 April 1835. Under a headline of 'Atrocious Murder' its article commences: *A very strong sensation has been excited here this week, by the report of the robbery and murder of an unfortunate female, of the name of Jean Brechin, between 40 and 50 years of age, who had spent the most of her life in the service of various respectable families in this neighbourhood.* It proceeds to inform its readers of Jane's shop, her marriage to John Adam in Laurencekirk, the sale and despatch of her furniture to Inverness, and her lodgings in Inverness. It then continues: *Adam, however, alone went to Dingwall; and all of a sudden he appeared possessed of money, although he had formerly been in poverty, so extreme, that he and a young woman, who lived with him as his wife, and was believed to be such, had been receiving assistance from the charitably disposed.* The article then concludes: *We abstain from entering further into detail. Adam however, has been secured, and is now lodged in Dingwall jail; and if it shall ultimately be established, as there seems little more room to doubt, that he is guilty of the foul act, a more deliberate deed of atrocity perhaps has not been perpetrated in Scotland since the days of Burke and Hare.*

John Adam was, of course, no longer in Dingwall jail. He had been taken to Inverness Tolbooth by John Macbean, escorted by a contingent of the Ross-shire militia. They had taken the route that crossed the Mulbuie, so that they would pass close by the ruined cottage where John had disposed of Jane's corpse in the anticipation that he might break down and confess. However, he seems to have studiously refused to look in the direction of the cottage. On arrival in Inverness, he had been admitted by the head jailor, William Fraser, and his turnkey, James McDonald. [These were the only jailors employed in Inverness Tolbooth. The head jailor was paid £40 per year and his assistant, known as the turnkey because he held the keys of the cells, was paid £20. The only other regular employee was the servant, whose job was to clean the cells and wash the bed linen. She was Elizabeth Alison, who was paid £5.]

Written confirmation of the successful transfer of John Adam to Inverness was forwarded to Procurator-Fiscal Hugh Cameron: *Upon the 17th day of April 1835 I, William Fraser, Head Jailor of Inverness, lawfully served the before named John Anderson or Adam with a full double of the foregoing petition, complaint and warrants thereon with a short copy of service thereto subjoined. This I did before these witnesses, James Macdonald and Alexander Dallas, both indwellers in Inverness.*

After the reporter from the *Inverness Journal*, John's next visitors at the Inverness Tolbooth were Jane Brechin's cousin, Margaret Munro (neé Garden) and her husband, Colin, from Montrose. After their declarations had been despatched to Dingwall from Montrose earlier in the week, the Procurator-Fiscal of Montrose, Robert Burness, had sent them by Mail coach to Inverness. They had arrived at midnight on Thursday 16 April. Archibald Gouk, the husband of Jane's sister, Mary, had also been sent to Inverness but there had not been a seat available on the coach. Next morning Margaret and Colin were taken by John Macbean to the Inverness Tolbooth where, in a 'line-up', they instantly recognised John Adam with no shadow of doubt as the person who had married Jane Brechin at her mother's house in Laurencekirk on Wednesday 11 March. They were also taken to Dingwall where, in the presence of the Procurator-Fiscal, they identified the chest of drawers, tent bed and trunk that had been carted from Montrose to John and Dorothy's lodgings in Dingwall.

They also identified the contents of the reticule clothes basket and square deal box as well as eighteen items that had been in the chest of drawers – including the pair of Derbyshire spar ornaments, which Margaret had specifically requested from Jane but which Jane had been particularly keen to take to Inverness. They also recognised the items of clothing that had been found on the corpse as those which Jane had been wearing when she and John had departed from Laurencekirk after their wedding.

That evening Archibald Gouk arrived in Inverness. He had secured a seat in the stagecoach that had departed Montrose the day after Margaret and Colin Munro had left. Next day (Saturday 18 April) he went to Dingwall where he provided a statement confirming that he was the person who had addressed Jane's letters to John Adam and identifying articles of Jane's clothing and furniture. He was then taken to the Tolbooth in Inverness where he readily pointed out John Adam.

Although his contribution to the murder precognition added little to the accumulating body of evidence, Archibald Gouk's testimony was the first (and only) to state that Jane Brechin's body had been interred. It is not clear exactly when or where this happened. The last record of anyone viewing the body was on Wednesday 15 April, which would also have been the date on which the three doctors last examined it – their reports having been received by the Procurator-Fiscal on Thursday 16 April. On being satisfied with these reports, he may have authorised immediate interment. It is certainly not recorded that Margaret or Colin Munro, who were in Dingwall on Friday 17 April, were offered the opportunity to view Jane's body. There also seems to be no reference in either the precognition papers or the Dingwall (St Clement's) old parish registers to where the body was buried. However, possible clues exist in the parish treasurer's records[45] in which an invoice covering the period March-May 1835 from a gravedigger named Simon McDonald itemises the digging of an anonymous grave [for all the other invoiced graves, the interred person is named]: *To digging a grave .... 1/6d.* A further invoice covering the same period – from a coffin maker, Donald Fraser – has also survived. It itemises names and exact dates of the burials for

Figure 26: St Clement's parish church, Dingwall

which he supplied coffins but there are none between 11 and 20 April. Thus it has to be assumed that Jane Brechin was probably buried coffin-less on Thursday 16 April 1835 within the graveyard of St Clement's parish church, Dingwall.

Public interest in the murder of Jane Brechin was now becoming widespread. For example, on Saturday 18 April both the *Caledonian Mercury*, published in Edinburgh, and the *Edinburgh Evening Courant* carried the identical 'Suspected Murder of a Wife by her Husband' article that had been published in the *Inverness Courier* on Wednesday 15 April.

The recording of the formal declarations of the various witnesses from Inverness continued apace during the period 17-20 April. Of prime significance were those of Hector and Janet MacIntosh, Jane's landlord and landlady in Chapel Street – undoubtedly the most influential of all the witnesses. Their account of the period between John and Jane's arrival in Inverness on 12 March and their departure from Inverness over the Kessock Ferry on 3 April, had provided crucial evidence of the circumstances leading up to the murder and their subsequent identification of Jane's corpse had provided the pivotal evidence leading to John Adam's arrest. Formal declarations were also received from: Robert Thomson – the carter whom John Adam had commissioned to transport Jane's furniture from North Kessock to Dingwall on Saturday 28 March; James Grant and his wife, Ann (neé Anderson); Ann Horack (neé Finister); and Mary Thomson (neé MacIntosh). The three ladies from Inverness had all been taken to Dingwall and had variously identified Jane's corpse and several items of her clothing – although Mary Thomson is revealed to have been less certain as she *thought the body resembled Jane, but could not comment on the clothes.*

Two further letters were received from Robert Burness, the Procurator-Fiscal of Montrose. One concerned the deposit and withdrawal of Jane's money from the Montrose branches of the National and British Linen Banks. Enclosed with this letter were the original countersigned deposit receipts, which David Hill and James Beattie had retrieved from their respective Head Offices.

The second letter contained the declarations of: John Younger – the Session Clerk of Montrose parish church who had arranged for the marriage banns to be read and the *usual certificate* to be issued; and Mary Gouk – the daughter of Archibald and Mary Gouk, who had brought Jane's letters to her father to be addressed to John Adam, c/o John Anderson in Dingwall. This second letter also contained a copy of a letter written to Robert Burness by Rev John Cook. Dated Sunday 19 April 1835, it explained that he had been away when a letter informing him of Jane Brechin's murder had arrived. On receiving the letter on his return he had immediately gone to visit Jane's mother, whom he described as *advanced in life*, and Jane's brother and sister [actually, sister-in-law], whom he described as *feeble of mind*. They had been in deep distress, having been informed of the murder by Robert Burness on the previous Friday [17 April]. Jane's mother had admitted to him that the marriage had taken place *much against her remonstrances ... as she knew little of him [John] and what she had heard was far from favourable* and that it must have been *only for the money that he was marrying her.*

It was not until Tuesday 21 April that Procurator-Fiscal Hugh Cameron formally interviewed Dorothy Elliott. It is not clear why he waited so long to take her evidence, except that she may have been too upset and confused about the events of the previous week to give a coherent account. Her revelations, however, were to have a profound impact on John Adam's defence. The following summary contains the main points from the 29-page declaration:

That she was 23 years old ... the daughter of Edward Elliott, a miner in the employ of John Bunting in Wirksworth, Derbyshire ... that she first met John Adam on Christmas Day 1833 in the house of Ralph Ordish, landlord of the Red Lion Inn, Derby, where she was an assistant cook ... that John Adam was a Private in the 2nd Dragoon Guards, billeted in the Red Lion Inn ... that when John Adam was removed to the Assizes in Duffield he visited her in plain clothes on leave of absence ... that he asked her to go to Scotland with him ... that her parents had disapproved but John had told her to tell them she was already married to him ... that a few days later she had agreed to go, on the assurance he would marry her in Sheffield ... that on their arrival in Sheffield John had postponed the marriage on account of no time – and still had not married her.

That they went from Sheffield to York and on to Edinburgh and Perth by Mail and by Defiance Stage Coach to a place from which they walked 5 miles to Craiggieloch farm occupied by his mother, near Alyth on Lord Airlie's estate ... that they stayed for a week ... that the farm was managed by John's brother, James ... that a sister, Janet, also lived there ... that John had introduced her as his wife ... that he wanted to leave as he was troubled by Biddy Esson by whom he had an illegitimate child.

That they travelled over the hills to Braemar and Tomintoul ... that in 8 or 9 days they arrived in Inverness ... that in Derby, John had about £60 in notes which he explained his mother had sent him in Derby and he had uplifted in a Bank in Glasgow where he had worked ... that he had given £20 to the mother of his child ... that in Inverness there was £10 left in £5 notes, one of Nottingham and one of Derby Banks ... that they were exchanged for two Bank of England notes in Inverness ... that it took 14 days ... that they had lodged with an old man, Mr Macdonald, in Gordon Place.

That they went to Dingwall where John expected to get work on a farm ... that they took lodging with John Urquhart, sawyer, where she still lived ... that John had got work in David Sutherland's quarry as a labourer ... that they went by the name of Anderson when in Dingwall ... that she was always supposed to be his lawful wife ... that John had assumed the name of Anderson as soon as they left Craiggieloch because he had another illegitimate child and was afraid of being followed ... that John's work had been suspended in winter ... that she was anxious about her situation and wanted to go home to her parents ... that John had told her they would not marry him in Dingwall ... that he had tried to borrow money from Sutherland so that she could return to England but had been refused ... that John had offered to go south to his brother to get money for the winter ... that he had returned 10 days later and given her 19/- ... that he had worked occasionally in the quarry until the middle of January.

That a letter had arrived for John ... that he told her he must go south to receive payment of a bequest by an uncle who had died in the West Indies ... that she had eventually persuaded John to let her read the letter ... that she was suspicious of the contents and the poor writing ... that it had been postmarked Montrose 4 February ... that John went south and said he would send her some money ... that when a letter arrived addressed to John Adam, c/o John Anderson she could not pay the postage ... that she asked that it be retained till John returned ... that some days later a letter arrived addressed to her ... that it contained a postal order for 20/- which she cashed ... that John returned in the 2nd week of March with a bundle, a new waistcoat and trousers and £100 in notes ... that he said the money was his share of what his father had left ... that furniture was coming by carrier which had been left by an aunt ... that John went to Inverness on two occasions to see if it had arrived ... that he had returned with a cart containing furniture.

That next week John worked in the quarry but was ill for most of the week ... that he went to Inverness supposedly to collect a basket that had been left there ... that he had returned late at night ... that he seemed stiff and tired which he said was because he had walked quickly and the basket was full ... that there was also an umbrella and bundle ... that the basket contained a pair of stockings, one unfinished with pins still in the loops, which surprised her ... that the items of clothes were marked IB ... that John said his aunt had married a man named Burns ... that there were also articles such as a tea caddy ... that she had not believed the story of the aunt and that she thought John must have bought them at a pawnbroker sale.

That on 10 April she had heard of the body ... that John had told her that people thought she must be the wife of a shepherd ... that she also recalled that John had told her about a cook in the same family of Mr Smart as he had served in Forfarshire ... that she was friendly with him and wanted to marry him ... that John had mentioned Brechin but as a place rather than a name.

That John had always been kind to her and tender-hearted but she had made up her mind to leave him to go home unless he married her ... that John had said she could go in May ... that he would follow her and marry her in England ... that she had been satisfied with that promise.

At the foot of her declaration it is stated by the Procurator-Fiscal that Dorothy Elliott *can write; but she is at present so agitated that she cannot sign her name.*

By co-incidence, that same day a letter from the War Office arrived at the Procurator-Fiscal's office in Dingwall. It informed that *two men from the 2nd Dragoon Guards had been despatched to Inverness to report to the Procurator-Fiscal for the purpose of identifying John Adam as a deserter from that Regiment since 18 March 1834 when they were in Derby.* A copy of the official Deserter Report[26] was attached.

A further letter from the Procurator-Fiscal of Montrose was also received that day. It explained that he had made enquiries about the letter that Jane Brechin had sent to John Adam in February 1835 but had been returned to the Dead Letter Office. Unfortunately, it had been destroyed so its contents would remain unknown. The Procurator-Fiscal's letter also enclosed a declaration from James Valentine, who had made John's wedding outfit and who had observed the large number of banknotes in John's pocket book.

Press reporters were still following the story and were quick to report the activities of the law officers and any other details as they emerged from the witness statements. On Wednesday 22 April the *Aberdeen Journal* re-ran the 'Atrocious Murder' article that had appeared in the *Montrose, Arbroath and Brechin Review* on Friday 17 April together with an abbreviated version of the 'Suspected Murder of a Wife by her Husband' article published by the *Inverness Courier* on Wednesday 15 April. The *Montrose, Arbroath and Brechin Review* on Friday 24 April also published some further particulars that had appeared in the *Inverness Courier* on Wednesday 15 April.

The *Inverness Journal* of Friday 24 April was the first to introduce some new detail to its readers. In an article headlined 'The late Murder in Ross-shire' it again showed its reporter's ability to interview prisoners in Inverness Tolbooth by announcing that John Adam had expressed *his decided conviction of being able to prove an alibi.* Its readers, however, were left to conjecture on the nature of this alibi, as no indication of its basis was supplied. The article also reports that the Procurator-Fiscal had visited John Adam along with a witness [un-named] from Montrose who had been present at his marriage with the deceased. This witness, after looking at John Adam, had said: *Oh John! I am sorry to see you here – don't you know me?* John had replied: *No, I know nothing about you.* The jailor then proceeded to take off John's night cap, so that the witness might more fully see his face and head. *Dinna do that,* said the witness, *I know him well enough, there is no doubt about it.* John Adam was said to have been unmoved, but had since *been almost constantly engaged in reading the Scriptures* – an observation that was to be consistently repeated throughout his remaining incarceration in Inverness Tolbooth.

Another article that provides fresh insights was published in the *Caledonian Mercury* on Saturday 25 April 1835. Whilst it acknowledges the *Inverness Courier* as its originator, it provides a lengthy, well-researched and journalistically superb account of the murder, describing it as *perhaps one of the most deliberate and atrocious cases of murder that ever stained the annals of our Scottish Courts of Justice. Guilt of so deep a dye is at all times striking and appalling, but in a remote secluded country, among a simple people, it awakes feelings of the utmost horror and amazement.* Proceeding to describe the hidden location of the corpse, it surmises that *it might have remained concealed for months or years (as the precise spot is rarely visited) but for the interposition of some such accident as that which led to the discovery.* Continuing to describe the discovery of the corpse and the extensive injuries inflicted by means of two large stones *covered with cloated blood,* the author postulates that these were *undoubtedly the instruments with which the murder was accomplished, and the whole might have been done so suddenly as to divest the unhappy victim of power to utter a scream.*

The account then queries the evidence of the probable date of the murder, stating that *the body lay undiscovered a week, and not a single night only as was supposed. Its fresh appearance deceived the medical gentlemen, but as it was completely secluded from the air, and covered by turf (which has an antiseptic quality), and the weather being chill, this appearance would probably have continued for more than eight days. This error as to the date of the murder is not the only mistake attending the different accounts of the transaction. The relatives of the deceased, who came from Montrose to identify the body, have given a different complexion to parts of the case, and as we have made diligent personal inquiries on the subject, both here and in Ross-shire, it will perhaps be better to put an end to the many absurd rumours afloat, as well as be more conducive to the ends of justice, to present our readers with a connected narrative of the facts as they have transpired.*

The article then provides an extensive account of how Jane had met John during their employment at Cairnbank during which they *got very intimate and were regarded as sweethearts*; how she had set up her shop in Montrose during which *the world seems to have gone prosperously with her*; how her *long-buried affection ... seems to have been stirred* by John Adam's marriage proposal; how her *ill fated marriage was solemnised by Mr Cook, the distinguished minister of Laurencekirk*; how she had lodged in Inverness awaiting John to *prepare a comfortable home for her*; how after the fateful crossing of the Kessock Ferry *she was never afterwards seen alive*. This, concluded the author poignantly, *ends the simple but melancholy story of Jane Brechin's life ... and her quiet unobtrusive existence, which seems to have been marked by only one indiscretion, her hasty and fatal marriage, terminated in the awful manner we have described.*

Turning its attentions to Dorothy Elliott, the article describes her as having *very pleasing manners and appearance ... artless simplicity of character and uniform propriety of conduct and her present situation as being pitiable in the extreme, and merits the sympathy of charitable minds.* However it considers her elopement into promised marriage with John Adam to have been *like many other damsels, doomed to experience the faithlessness of such pledges.* Continuing to adopt this morally-critical Presbyterian viewpoint, the article develops a reproachful opinion of her behaviour: *The folly and disobedience of this poor girl, in quitting her parent's roof, and rushing into so rash and dangerous connection, has plunged her in a depth of sorrow, destitution and disgrace, that she can never wholly emerge from. The recollection of the past will haunt her through life, and poison all her future existence.*

The final paragraph of (in its own words) *the preceding too lengthened statement* takes the opportunity to heap praise on the *great activity and zeal of the local authorities* concluding that *few murders have ever been committed under circumstances of more cold-blooded determination and cruelty; and very few, where the crime was hid by so thick a cloud of darkness, have so soon been brought to light.*

After two weeks of hectic activity since the discovery of the corpse on Friday 10 April, the Procurator-Fiscal's office during the last week in April appears to have been relatively tranquil. This may have been because Hugh Cameron himself was in Edinburgh discussing the progress of his precognition with officers of the High Court of Justiciary to gain their acceptance that the evidence against John Adam was strong and to ensure that a trial would be scheduled into the autumn diet of the Circuit Court in Inverness.

It was not until Thursday 30 April that Sergeant James Bleakley and Private Joseph Collier of the 2nd Dragoon Guards arrived in Inverness. They were immediately taken to the Tolbooth where, in the presence of Hugh Cameron, they identified John Adam as the deserter they had been sent to find. Once again, a reporter from the *Inverness Journal* appears to have been present. On Friday 1 May 1835 he wrote that John Adam cordially shook hands with the two soldiers, inquired where the regiment was stationed and asked after some of his old companions. He also reported that John *is cheerful and talks familiarly with his fellow prisoners.* Two weeks later, on Friday 15 May, the *Montrose, Arbroath & Brechin Review* carried the same story, emphasising that John still *continues to assert that he is innocent of the crime and denied that John Adam, Montrose, and John Anderson, Dingwall, was the same person.* As events would turn out, this news was seriously out of date by the time it was published.

It is not clear when the two soldiers from the 2nd Dragoon Guards departed Inverness but they seem to have carried the news that John was in civil custody back to the Regiment (at that time billeted in Ipswich). Subsequently, the Register of Army Deserters[27] became annotated: *Not apprehended!!!* [presumably meaning that he had not been apprehended by the Army]. To this day, the space allocated for an entry against the reference number (57269) in the Register of Captured Deserters[28] remains blank.

Until he was identified by the visiting soldiers as an Army deserter, John Adam had vigorously refused to acknowledge his enlistment in the 2nd Dragoon Guards, for example in his declarations of 14 and 16 April. He had also adhered to his name being John Anderson, not John Adam, and had resolutely denied any marriage to Jane Brechin or knowing any of the witnesses from Montrose. However, by early May 1835, he must have begun to realise that the weight of evidence being gathered by the authorities was overwhelming and that he could no longer sustain his alias or the previous explanations of his activities. He therefore offered to provide a 3rd declaration – one that was much nearer the truth. It was taken on Thursday 7 May by Hugh Cameron in the presence of William Fraser Tytler, the Sheriff of the County of Inverness. The following is a summary of the main points contained within the 20-page declaration:

That his name is John Adam, not John Anderson ... that he is a native of Lintrathen parish ... that his father was the tenant of Campsie farm in said parish, then Craigieloch where his mother is still tenant ... that he once served for six months as servant to Mr Crichton in Cupar Angus, but never was a farm servant in England ... that in 1831 he enlisted in Glasgow in the 2nd Dragoon Guards and went to England, where he was stationed in various places until 1834.

That on 18/19 March at Duffield in Derby he deserted and came to Scotland with Dorothy Elliott whom he induced to accompany him and promised to marry ... that they travelled by Craigieloch and then to Inverness and Dingwall ... that he had not formally married

Dorothy ... that the money (about £50) was savings before he enlisted ... that he was employed in Dingwall but from Martinmas he had gone to Montrose to get repayment of money (about £80) he had lent to Jane Brechin who had a grocery shop in Castle Street, before he joined the Dragoons ... that she had been a servant to William Smart at Cairnbank, near Montrose.

That he and Jane were 'in terms of marriage' ... that she had told him she would not repay the money until he returned from enlistment to marry her ... that they arranged to be married in March ... that he was absent from Dingwall for nine days and gave no information to Dorothy on his return ... that he returned to Montrose for about 14 days ... that Jane disposed of her effects but reserved a chest of drawers, a trunk and a bed which were taken by carrier to Aberdeen and then to Inverness.

That he married Jane in Laurencekirk on 11 March at her mother's house ... that Rev Cook carried out the service ... that they then travelled to Aberdeen and Inverness by Defiance coach ... that Jane carried a clothes basket and umbrella ... that Jane gave him two deposit receipts: one from the British Linen Co. for £93 or £96; the other from the National Bank for £15 ... that he cashed these and gave Jane £5 or £7 and kept the remainder.

That on arrival in Inverness on 12 March he had gone to Fraser's public house where he had been pointed to the house next door ... that he left by Mail to Dingwall ... that he did not tell Dorothy of his movements or marriage but had told her, as in his first declaration, of his legacy and his share of his father's succession ... that he deposited £100 in the bank in Dingwall ... that he returned to Jane next day, dined and returned to Dingwall ... that on the next Saturday, or the one after, he went to Inverness to enquire about the arrival of Jane's furniture ... that he hired a cart to the ferry and had it carried to Dingwall by Mr Thomson ... that he told Dorothy that the furniture had been bequeathed by his aunt ... that the next time he was in Inverness was to see Mr George Wilson and that he went to see Jane who said her lodgings were cold and that she wanted to leave ... that they went to the windmill near the Kessock Ferry where he left Jane ... that she was to write to him about where she would *be lodging ... that he had never seen her since, unless the corpse was hers ... that it was much disfigured and could not say.*

That she was dressed in a black velvet bonnet, veil, mantle and thick gown similar to those on display ... that the initials 'JB' were Jane's ... that the reticule basket that she was carrying held worsted stockings she was making, one being unfinished ... that he was to keep them until she could finish them ... that he gave them to Dorothy telling her his mother had started them ... that in the bundle he carried to the ferry were a blue coat, black trousers and a black and white vest ... that the coat, vest and a pair of brown trousers that he was now wearing were his wedding clothes.

The statement was witnessed and signed by Hugh Innes Cameron (Procurator-Fiscal), Donald Mackenzie (Sheriff Clerk Depute), John Macbean (Messenger-at-Arms) and William Austin (Clerk).

Thus John continued to deny the murder, now claiming that he had not seen Jane since they had parted at the Kessock ferry. However, under the pressure of evidence from the Montrose and Inverness witnesses, he had now admitted his true surname, his desertion from the Army and his marriage to Jane Brechin. These new admissions now switched the focus of the Procurator-Fiscal's precognition onto the witnesses from the Black Isle and Dingwall, in the hope that their evidence would clarify John Adam's movements during and after the presumed night of the murder.

Although the date is not recorded, Hugh Cameron commissioned George Campbell Smith, a surveyor from Banff, to prepare a map of the murder scene[46]. The map, which is dated 9 May 1835 and is entitled *Sketch of the Site of Ground about the House in which the Dead Body of Jane Brechin was found on 10th April 1835*, was based on the Reduced Plan of the Survey of the Commons of Mulbuy, Cromarty, etc[47] drawn by Peter Brown in 1816 when the commonty of the Mulbuie was divided up amongst the landowners of the area. It shows that there were two old cottages, the south-east corner of the northern one being where Jane Brechin's corpse was found. It was 279 yards from Macdonald's public house [the ½-way house] on the parliamentary road from Scuddel to Kessock and Fortrose, and 462 yards from William Forbes' house at Muckernich. [Although the cottages are marked on both the 1st edition (1873) and 2nd edition (1905) Ordnance Survey maps[48], they are not marked on modern maps and there are no longer any visible remains due to modern forestry operations.]

Throughout the first half of May, several more declarations were received. That of Ronald Gordon, teller in the National Bank branch in Dingwall, confirmed that John Anderson (Adam) had deposited £100 on Friday 13 March and had withdrawn it again on Friday 10 April. He also affirmed that he had witnessed the discovery of John's pocket book containing £74, including the 20/- John Maberly & Co. banknote, and the receipt from John Macdonald for £20 as security against the hire of a horse, dated Friday 10 April. The declaration of John Urquhart confirmed that John and Dorothy were his lodgers – but he was unable to accurately recall the dates on which John had left Dingwall for his visits to Montrose or Inverness. Also, he was confused about the date on which John had departed with the horse, suggesting that it might have been Friday 3 April. His wife, Christine, and daughter, Jane, were also unable to confirm this date. These uncertainties over crucial dates would later afford John's defence an opportunity to offer an alibi.

Another person who supplied a declaration (on Friday 15 May) was David Sutherland, the Craig Quarry tenant who had employed John Anderson (Adam). He confirmed the various requests John had made for loans and what he knew of the occasions John had departed for the South. He also explained the irregular nature of the work he had been able to offer John and produced a detailed statement of account for the days on which John had worked between June 1834 and April 1835. This showed that John had last been paid on 19 February 1835 and that he had worked 3 days in April 1835 for which he was still due 5/8d in wages.

Declarations were also received from: Alexander Macleay – the carpenter who, in company with Thomas Ross from Dingwall, had crossed the Kessock Ferry with John and had conversed about his

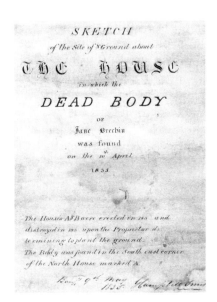

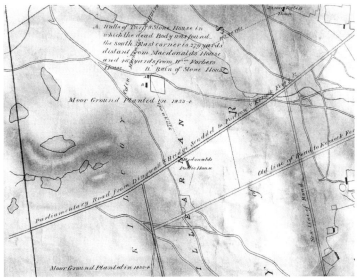

Figure 27: George Campbell Smith's map of the murder site (reproduced with permission of Alasdair Cameron, Muir of Ord)

work in the quarry; and Roderick Hay – the Dingwall postmaster, who had put Jane Brechin's second letter to John in the post office window and had subsequently sent it to the Dead Letter Office.

On Monday 18 May 1835, Procurator-Fiscal Hugh Cameron sent an initial handwritten 'Schedule of Precognition' to David Cleghorn, a Crown Agent whose offices in Edinburgh were at 38 Castle Street, and who had been appointed by the Lord Advocate to prepare the case for the prosecution of John Adam in the High Court of Justiciary. The schedule[49] stated the key dates:

Date of warrants of commitment for further examination, 14 April;
Date of warrant of commitment to jail, 16 April;
Date of commitment to Inverness jail, 16 April;
Dates of declarations of accused, 14/16 April and 7 May;
Date of precognition, 15 May;
Date of forwarding of precognition to Crown Agent, 18 May.

Attached to the schedule was a covering letter stating: *I send herewith precognition and relevant documents, consisting of 17 numbers as per Inventory ... (which) contains the investigation I have made into the circumstances of a horrid murder committed near the Parliamentary road leading from Dingwall to Inverness ... John Adam, taken into custody on suspicion of being guilty, has emitted three judicial declarations and for greater security has been committed prisoner to the Tolbooth in Inverness.*

In Scotland, all public prosecutions are conducted by the Crown Office and the Procurator-Fiscal Service, nominally in the name of the 'Lord Advocate', who is the chief law officer and the chief public prosecutor for the Crown for both civil and criminal matters. The 'Solicitor General' for Scotland is a Deputy to the Lord Advocate, with the particular duty of advising the Crown on matters of Scots Law. 'Crown Counsel' is the collective name for the Lord Advocate, Solicitor General and Advocates Depute. 'Crown Agents' advise the Lord Advocate on prosecution matters and act for the Lord Advocate in all High Court proceedings. Crown Agents also issue general instructions about prosecutions for Procurators-Fiscal, Sheriffs and other public officials and, in consultation with the 'Clerk of Justiciary', arrange sittings of the High Court of Justiciary.

Next day, Tuesday 19 May, Hugh Cameron also sent a copy of the precognition schedule and its attachments to John Jardine, the Sheriff of Ross & Cromarty. In his covering letter he raised the issue of the exact date of the murder: *The greatest discrepancy between the witnesses is the date of the murder – that is of the departure of Adam and Jane Brechin from their lodgings. Inverness witnesses all state the date to have been Friday 3 April and Dingwall witnesses and John Adam make the day he was last in Inverness and last from home as Monday 30 March. I have no doubt that the latter is the true date and in the evening of that day the unfortunate woman was deprived of life.* Why Hugh Cameron should have preferred Monday 30 March over the much more plausible Friday 3 April is unexplained, but the issue of the true date of the murder would arise on several more occasions over the next few months – and would give John Adam the opportunity to construct a plausible defence.

On Wednesday 20 May, John Jardine, Sheriff of Ross & Cromarty, handed copies of the precognition documents to John Shaw-Stewart, Lord Moncrieff, the Solicitor General and Advocate-Depute, who had travelled to Dingwall to discuss the case with the Sheriff and the Procurator-Fiscal. Included with the papers were copies of two further declarations that had been sent by Robert Burness, the Procurator-Fiscal of Montrose, and had just arrived in Dingwall. Both of these had been taken by James Spence, the Provost of Brechin, but were of little consequence to the investigation.

The first was a declaration from James Henton, a maltman at the Glencadam distillery in Brechin. He was a cousin of John Adam who had visited him last winter. During the visit John had informed him that he had been a soldier and had married an English woman who had money and had paid for his discharge – the same story that John had told when he and Dorothy had stayed at Craigieloch in March/April 1834 before departing over the hills to Inverness. The revelation that John Adam had been 'discharged' from the Army had not been information contained in any of the previous declarations from the Forfarshire witnesses. Robert Burness was not aware that two soldiers from the 2nd Dragoon Guards had already identified John Adam as a deserter, so he had sent this declaration to Dingwall in the expectation that it was also new information there. The second declaration was from David Hershell, a merchant in Brechin, whose sister was married to James Adam, now a toll gatherer at the Jellybrands Toll between Stonehaven and Aberdeen [Taylor & Skinner's 1776 road map[50] refers to an Inn named 'Jeally Brans' on this road]. Presumably, he had read the reports in the Montrose, Arbroath and Brechin Review and had come forward to divulge that John and James Adam were second cousins who had been fellow servants at Cairnbank for about 18 months in 1827-28.

On Thursday 21 May, Sheriff Jardine of Ross & Cromarty wrote to David Cleghorn, the Crown Agent in Edinburgh. The letter refers to Advocate-Depute John Shaw-Stewart, *with whom I had some conversation today on the case of the Millbuie murder – the most interesting and important that has for many years occurred in that quarter – [who] is anxious to have it before him as soon as possible.* [This was the first indication that the Advocate-Depute John Shaw-Stewart, Lord Moncrieff, would be the judge at the ensuing trial.] Sheriff Jardine then raises the situation of Dorothy Elliott – *the girl from England with whom Adam held as his wife at Dingwall. Mr Cameron informs that she is at present maintained at his expense. Mr Stewart Mackenzie has applied to her parish in Derbyshire to take her back – but you will consider whether you will authorise Mr Cameron to continue her maintenance in this country until the trial, and when you return the precognitions to him you will give him your directions accordingly.*

No letters from David Cleghorn, the Crown Agent in Edinburgh, responding either to the precognition papers sent on 18 May or to the Sheriff's letter sent on Thursday 21 May seem to have survived. However, a copy of the covering letter sent to him with the precognition papers is contained in the trial papers and it is annotated with David Cleghorn's comments dated Tuesday 26 May: *Let the MDs [medical doctors] state with more precision the cause of death,*

Figure 28: John Jardine, Sheriff of Ross & Cromarty
(from John Kay's Originals, Vol 2, No CCCXXVII)

viz the particular injuries upon the head, which were followed by fatal consequences. Let them also point out the probable sort of implement with which they were inflicted, and especially let them say whether from the position, nature and number of the injuries, they infer that they must have been inflicted by the hand of another, or whether it is possible that they have been caused by an accident such as the falling of the wall upon the deceased when asleep within the place where she was found. [Also] I wish to have someone who (besides the Fiscal) was present when the body was shown to the different persons who identified it, who may prove that it was the same body which was found in the old building.

This was the first occasion on which a fresh mind had been applied to the evidence collected by the Dingwall-based prosecuting authorities. The points raised were certainly quite perceptive in identifying possible avenues of defence for John Adam. The second point – that the body found at the Heights of Kilcoy might not have been the same body as that laid out in the Town House in Dingwall – could no longer be irrefutably proven, because Jane was already interred and no witnesses (other than the doctors) to the identity of the body in Dingwall had been present at the site of its discovery. Conversely, no person who had been present at the discovery of the body had been called to identify it in Dingwall. However, there was one detail that Hugh Cameron could bring to bear. The murder handbill had not stated that Jane was missing a front tooth [lost only a few months before her death], yet three witnesses had noted this in their declarations – Janet MacIntosh and Ann Anderson from Inverness, and Margaret Munro from Montrose]. If they had not seen the same body, they could not have pointed this out. Nowadays, it is a common tactic for police to withhold a piece of information so that evidence can later be authenticated – perhaps Hugh Cameron had not made a mistake and should be accredited for his foresight.

The first point in David Cleghorn's annotations – that the death could have been a simple accident caused by heavy stones falling during the collapse of the wall of the derelict cottage – was pertinent because no evidence had been found to link John Adam with the site of the discovery of the body. Hugh Cameron tackled this point on Saturday 30 May by re-interviewing John Jones and William Hill, the doctors who had carried out the post-mortem. They confirmed that there were two lacerate head wounds which could each have caused death. One was on the upper part of the parietal bone, and the other was on the right side of the same bone towards the back part of the head [parietal bones are the bones in the human skull which collectively form the cranium]. Both wounds were about one inch in depth and both had *cut through the pericranium*. The violence of the blow under the right ear had fractured the lower jaw bone on both sides. It had been caused by a blunt instrument, bludgeon or stone – and the large stone removed from near the head, if thrown down upon her head where she lay, could have produced the injury to the ear and both injuries to the jaw. They concluded that *the quantity of turf, sand and stones would have been sufficient to suffocate – but appearances would have been different on dissection. Therefore, in their opinion, the injuries could not have been self-inflicted, as the walls of the hut would not have fallen of themselves.* These declarations, together with the declarations of the two witnesses from Brechin and a supplementary precognition schedule, were despatched by Hugh Cameron to David Cleghorn on Monday 1 June.

The plight of Dorothy Elliott again came to the fore during the last week of May and the first week of June 1835 when, once again, the *Inverness Journal* showed its prowess at watching the comings and goings at the Inverness Tolbooth. On Friday 29 May it carried an account, headed 'The Mulbuie Murder', detailing a visit to John's cell made by Dorothy on Wednesday 27 May. Although it is probable that Dorothy had made previous visits to John, this was their first recorded meeting since John had been taken into custody on Monday 13 April:

The unfortunate pair shook hands, and the female, who appears to be a respectable person, wept bitterly; she did not upbraid the prisoner. He protested he was innocent of the crime laid to his charge, and expressed his decided conviction that he should be acquitted, adding that, if in his power, he would force on his trial before the autumn assizes. The young woman said it was much to be regretted that he had not at once admitted his marriage with the deceased; to which Adam replied, 'that can't now be helped.' He inquired eagerly how she supported herself, and if any person lived in the house with her. She said that she resided alone – that the benevolence of Provost Cameron of Dingwall made her want for nothing. He seemed gratified at this, and added, 'Oh! As soon as the trial is over, I shall join the regiment with which I was connected.' The female observed that, until the result of the trial, she would no more visit him, but she would write frequently, and send him clean clothes. Adam, during this conversation, appeared cheerful; his visitor, however, was much distressed, and left him, saying, 'John, I forgive you for what you have done to me; may the Almighty forgive you – farewell!'

The article then concludes with the statement that: *Adam, alias Anderson*, devotes the greater part of his time to reading the Bible. This was the second occasion on which the *Inverness Journal* had noted that John Adam had re-kindled his interest with Christian religious thinking. This was not because he had become a believer – he was a Deist who was fascinated with what he regarded as the futility of religious belief and practice. His new-found desire to understand Christianity, even if he didn't practice it, would emerge more frequently in the ensuing months.

Presumably because of its human interest, the *Inverness Journal's* article was reproduced under the same 'Mulbuie Murder' headline in the *Montrose, Arbroath & Brechin Review* on Friday 5 June and in the *Caledonian Mercury* on Saturday 6 June. Dorothy's comment in that article – that she wanted for nothing – was not quite true. Although the Procurator-Fiscal had been paying her rent, she was relying on charity for her maintenance. She had previously received money from the Poor Fund in February 1835 and an entry in the Dingwall Kirk Session Poor Roll Account[32] of June 1835 itemises a further payment of 5/- made to *Mrs Anderson in distress*. From Dorothy's comments about sending clean clothes to John and not visiting him until after the trial, it can also be surmised that it had been agreed by the Procurator-Fiscal and the Crown Agent that Dorothy could return to her parents in Derbyshire, at least for the time being.

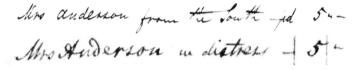

Figure 29: Two entries of payments to Dorothy Elliott (Mrs Anderson) in the Dingwall Poor Rolls of February and June 1835 (reproduced with permission of the Church of Scotland)

The pace of the investigation was now less hectic. What remained to be done in preparation for the impending trial was to complete the taking of statements from the remaining potential witnesses and to collect any further evidence that might help to reveal John Adam's movements at the time of the murder or might directly link him to the murder scene.

One avenue of investigation initiated by Hugh Cameron was to request Robert Burness in Montrose to arrange for the contents of the 'band box' left by John and Dorothy at Craigieloch in March/April 1834 to be procured. Robert Burness raised the issue with William Hutchison, the Procurator-Fiscal of Forfarshire, who then procured a warrant to search Craigieloch. On Tuesday 23 June, William Hutchison, accompanied by John Stewart, a Forfarshire Sheriff's officer, called on 'widow Adam' at Craigieloch. She produced the band box – but it was empty. Apparently the contents had been taken away by John and Dorothy when they had left. A search of the house was carried out by the Sheriff's officer but nothing that might have belonged to John or Dorothy was found. The band box was removed by William Hutchison and taken to Robert Burness in Montrose, who took formal declarations from each of the two men.

These two declarations were despatched to Hugh Cameron on Saturday 27 June, along with an account for expenses of £4-17-4d and a covering letter which explained that the band box had been retained in Montrose as it was presumed to be *of no importance*. This despatch also contained a declaration from William Barclay, Jane Brechin's cousin in Montrose, which had been taken by Provost John Barclay of Montrose on Monday 22 June. He confirmed that in 1832 his father had addressed two letters from Jane Brechin to John Adam, who at that time was stationed in Piercehill Barracks, Edinburgh. He also confirmed that in September 1834 Jane had purchased a pair of men's shoes, which John Adam had worn on a visit in November of that year.

On Tuesday 30 June, Hugh Cameron forwarded the three declarations from Montrose to David Cleghorn, the Crown Agent in Edinburgh. He also forwarded the statement of account that David Sutherland had produced on Friday 15 May, showing that John Adam had worked for only three days during April 1835. By John's own declaration, these working days had been 6, 7 and 8th April.

These dates were of importance to Hugh Cameron in his efforts to establish John's whereabouts on the days leading up to the murder and prior to the discovery of the corpse on Friday 10 April. He was also able to pinpoint a further date by taking declarations from Kenneth and Ann Mackenzie. They confirmed that their young daughter, Helen, had died on Saturday 28 March and had been buried on Monday 30 March. Dorothy Elliott had attended the funeral but John had not attended because he was ill and at home in bed. This information was transmitted to David Cleghorn on Wednesday 8 July

Somewhat surprisingly, on Tuesday 7 July a short article entitled 'The Millbuie Murder' was published in *The Times*. It had failed to carry any news of the murder on any previous occasion, so why it chose 7 July to start informing its readers is unclear. Perhaps it had noted that the schedule for the Circuit Court in Inverness had been announced and had included the expected date of the trial of John Adam (Friday 18 September).

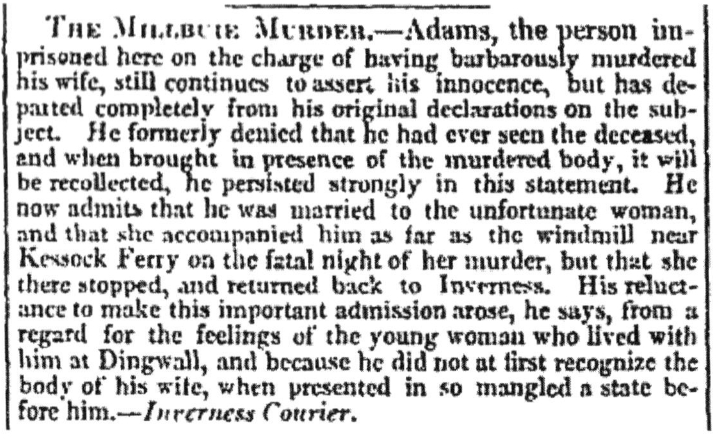

THE MILLBUIE MURDER.—Adams, the person imprisoned here on the charge of having barbarously murdered his wife, still continues to assert his innocence, but has departed completely from his original declarations on the subject. He formerly denied that he had ever seen the deceased, and when brought in presence of the murdered body, it will be recollected, he persisted strongly in this statement. He now admits that he was married to the unfortunate woman, and that she accompanied him as far as the windmill near Kessock Ferry on the fatal night of her murder, but that she there stopped, and returned back to Inverness. His reluctance to make this important admission arose, he says, from a regard for the feelings of the young woman who lived with him at Dingwall, and because he did not at first recognize the body of his wife, when presented in so mangled a state before him.—*Inverness Courier.*

Figure 30: The short report of the murder published by *The Times* on 7 July 1835

Whilst acknowledging its source, the article carried by *The Times* was in reality only an abbreviated and edited version of an article published by the *Inverness Courier* on Wednesday 1 July (and by the *Arbroath, Montrose & Brechin Review* on Friday 10 July): *Adam, the person imprisoned here on the charge of having barbarously murdered his wife, has relinquished all intention of forcing on his trial and will wait the decision of the Circuit Court of Justiciary in September. He still continues to assert his innocence, but has departed from his original declarations on the subject. He formerly denied that he had ever seen the deceased, and when brought in presence of the murdered body, it will be recollected, he persisted strongly in this statement. He now admits that he was married to the unfortunate woman, and that she accompanied him as far as the windmill near Kessock Ferry on the fatal night of her murder, but that she there stopped, and returned back to Inverness. His reluctance to make this important admission arose, he says, from a regard for the feelings of the young woman who lived* with him at Dingwall, and because he did not at first recognize the body of his wife, when presented in so mangled a state before him. His confinement has in some measure reduced his athletic appearance, but he is healthy and cheerful and reads frequently at his Bible. He complained grievously to us one day of the heavy irons on his body, and wished to have them taken off for a part of the day, that he might be allowed to walk about the passage in front of his cell. This reasonable request has since been complied with.

As previously, no correspondence from David Cleghorn, the Crown Agent in Edinburgh, responding to the declarations forwarded by Hugh Cameron on Tuesday 30 June and Wednesday 8 July seems to have survived. However, a copy of the covering letter sent to him with the declarations of William Hutchison and John Stewart is contained in the trial papers and it is annotated with David Cleghorn's comments dated Friday 31 July: *It is desirable to free the evidence from some discrepancy which exists as to dates. There seems no reason to doubt that it was on Monday 6 April, he [John Adam] left Inverness with her [Jane Brechin] and murdered her. I think the above object will be in a great measure effected by fixing with precision the Saturday on which the furniture was taken to Dingwall. The carter and the ferryman do not agree as to this day, which John Adam says was within 21-28 March.*

Examine the Elgin carrier, who probably will know on which day the furniture was delivered by him – and Mr Laidlaw's servant may throw some light on the point. Was Kenneth Mackenzie's child buried on the 30th [March] or 6th [April]? Has Donald Fraser's brother-in-law been examined? ['Mr Laidlaw's servant' was a possible witness who had been named by Roderick MacGregor, the ferryman. He worked for a Mr Laidlaw of Contin and had a horse and cart at the Kessock Ferry when John was negotiating transport of Jane's furniture. John, of course, had ignored Mr Laidlaw's servant because he did not want the furniture to be taken to Contin. He had said he wanted the furniture taken to Contin, but this was to ensure that it would not be carted away before he had time to remove Jane's clothes from the chest. 'Donald Fraser's brother-in-law' had been mentioned by John Urquhart as possibly being the Duncan Macdonald who had accompanied John

Adam from the Kessock ferry to Dingwall on Thursday 12 March and who had taken a drink with him in the ½-way Inn.]

The Fiscal will revise the Inventory to see particularly whether it includes the clothes found on the body. He will also send an accurate list of the articles, furniture, baskets, etc which are not yet included in it. I suggest anything which occurs to him as to be produced or otherwise.

I have not libelled on the sealed pocket book, understanding that it contains only the bank notes and the paper regarding the horse.

D. Elliott's evidence and that of the Urquharts would lead to the belief that Monday 30 March was the day, but the statement of H. MacIntosh that they remained 3 weeks and 3 days brings it to 6th April and this along with John Adam's statement that it was the Monday night after the furniture was home (supposing this to have been the 28th) leads me to suppose that the above witnesses have mistaken the time by a week.

It seems that David Cleghorn must have written these annotations prior to his receipt of the information that Helen Mackenzie was buried on Monday 30 March, otherwise he would not have needed to ask the question. Furthermore, the date of the murder – which was originally thought to be only one or two days before the discovery of the body because of its fresh appearance – had previously been queried by the *Caledonian Mercury* report of Saturday 25 April 1835. This report had pointed out that the temperature of the ground and the exclusion of air had made the body look fresher than it actually was and that it had probably lain at the Heights of Kilcoy for a week. David Cleghorn's reasoning that the body had lain for only four days relied exclusively on the surmise that Hector MacIntosh's account for Jane's accommodation in Inverness should have been for two weeks and three days. Why he should have thought that a miscalculation by one week was any more likely than three days is difficult to understand – especially as the latter would have concurred with the unanimity of the witnesses who stated that it was on Friday 3 April that John and Jane departed Inverness and crossed the Kessock ferry, making this the true date of the murder. Furthermore, David Cleghorn also seems to have neglected the fact that John, supported by his employer, David Sutherland, had an indisputable alibi for Monday 6 April – he was working at the quarry.

There is no evidence that Hugh Cameron tried to interview '*Mr Laidlaw's servant*' or '*Donald Fraser's brother-in-law*' but he did take declarations from John Murdoch, the carrier who had transported Jane's furniture from Elgin to Inverness, and Nicol Mackenzie, his porter. They were able to confirm that they had carried the furniture but were not able to provide an exact date for its arrival in Inverness. Hugh Cameron also interviewed Duncan Macdonald, the quarrier at the Bruichnain quarry, who had crossed the Beauly Firth on the Kessock ferry with John Adam when he had first left Jane Brechin in her lodgings in Chapel Street, Inverness. He thought that crossing had been on Monday 16 March – although it was actually Thursday 12 March, the evening before John deposited £100 in the National Bank in Dingwall. These three declarations were forwarded to David Cleghorn on Friday 7 August and they turned out to be the final witness declarations of the precognition.

In total, 59 witnesses had been examined and their testimonies were amassed into a precognition package of 427 handwritten pages[44.]

CHAPTER SEVEN

Trial

The trial of John Adam had now been arranged to take place at the Inverness Circuit of the High Court of Justiciary on Friday 18 September 1835. With the precognition complete, the preparations for the trial were now put in hand. These included the formulation of the indictment, the finalisation of the list of witnesses and the creation of inventories of clothing, furniture and other articles to be annexed to the indictment. But first, the matter of the actual date of the murder still had to be settled.

After receiving David Cleghorn's latest annotations referring to the date of the murder, Hugh Cameron responded in a letter dated Tuesday 11 August. This letter confirmed the view that he had previously expressed in the letter he had sent to Sheriff John Jardine of Ross & Cromarty on Tuesday 19 May in which he had favoured Monday 30 March as the date of the murder. In justifying this view he wrote: *John Adam and Jane Brechin arrived on [Thursday] 12 March. Hector MacIntosh states they were in his house 3 weeks and 3 days and left on [Friday] 3 April. 3 weeks and 3 days takes to [Monday] 6 April ... the MacIntoshes overcalculated by 1 week ... but 2 weeks and 3 days from [Thursday] 12 March makes it to [Monday] 30 March.* It is difficult to understand why Hugh Cameron persisted with the extraordinary illogicality of this argument, when it was quite clear that the MacIntoshes had over-calculated by 3 days, thus arriving at Friday 3 April as the date of John and Jane's departure – as stated by all the Inverness witnesses.

This letter of Tuesday 11 August was contained in a package which included a supplementary schedule of the precognition which, in addition to the dates contained in the initial schedule, recorded four additional key dates:

Date of receipt of precognition from Crown Agent, 3 August;

Date of 1st additional step, 3 August;

Date of last step in proceedings, 11 August;

Date of re-transmitting to Crown Agent, 11 August.

The package also contained: the proposed indictment; a revised list of witnesses from Inverness and Dingwall; a list of the deceased's body clothes; a list of the articles libelled on; a list of other articles identified by witnesses but not libelled on; and a list of articles not identified. On the same day, Robert Burness submitted the list of witnesses from Montrose. Thus all the necessary documentation for the preparation of the trial papers was in the hands of the Crown Agent and Advocate-Depute in Edinburgh by mid-August. [In Scottish law, the term 'libelled on' does not refer to defamation but to the grounds, stated in an indictment, on which the charge against an accused is brought to a criminal court.]

Documents relating to the trial and its preliminaries are contained in the collection of trial papers[51]. The first pre-trial document, issued on Monday 24 August 1835 in the name of King William IV by the Advocate General, was the Letter of Diligence[52] authorising the Circuit Court of Justiciary to try John Adam and summonsing the witnesses to appear *within the Criminal Courthouse of Inverness* on 18 September 1835 *under the pain of One Hundred Merks Scots.*

The second document, issued on Monday 24 August 1835 by John Shaw-Stewart, the Advocate-Depute, was the Indictment[53] served on John Adam. As defence advocates were not permitted to read the precognitions on which indictments were based, this was a document particularly awaited by James Crawford, who had been appointed by the Advocate-General as John's defence counsel. In effect, he had been given a generous period of twenty-five days in which to construct John's defence – the obligatory period in 1835 being fifteen days. It reads:

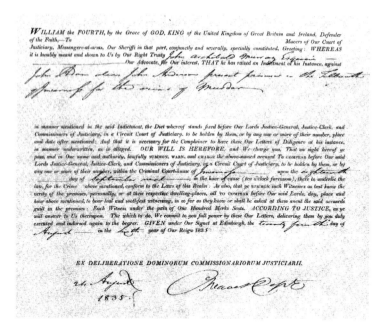

Figure 31: King William IV's letter of diligence authorising the Circuit Court of Justiciary to try John Adam for the murder of Jane Brechin (National Records of Scotland)

JOHN ADAM alias JOHN ANDERSON, present prisoner in the tollbooth of Inverness, you are Indicted and Accused at the instance of JAMES ARCHIBALD MURRAY, Esquire, his Majesty's [Lord] Advocate, for his Majesty's interest: THAT ALBEIT, by the laws of this and of every other well governed realm, MURDER is a crime of a heinous nature, and severely punishable: YET TRUE IT IS AND OF VERITY, that you the said John Adam alias John Anderson are guilty of the said crime, actor, or art and part: IN SO FAR AS,

On or about the 30th day of March 1835,

or on or about the 6th day of April 1835,

or on one or other of the days of these months, or of February immediately preceding, or of May immediately following, the particular day being to the Prosecutor unknown, at a place in or near

118

to a plantation on the lands of Kilcoy, or on the heights or braes of Kilcoy, in the parish of Killearnan, and shire of Ross, which place is distant two hundred and eighty yards or thereby in a north-easterly direction from the house situated at the heights or braes of Kilcoy aforesaid, then and now or lately occupied by Alexander Macdonald, then and now or lately changekeeper there, or at some place in the vicinity thereof to the Prosecutor unknown, you the said John Adam alias John Anderson did wickedly and feloniously attack and assault Jean [Jane] Brechin, shortly before then residing in or near Montrose, who was then your wife, or at least with whom you had a short time previously entered into a matrimonial connection; and you did, with a stone or some other hard instrument to the Prosecutor unknown, strike her two or thereby violent blows on the head, whereby she was severely cut or wounded on the head, and was stunned, and you did then violently strike or dash down upon the side of her head a large stone. Or some other hard and heavy substance to the Prosecutor unknown, whereby the jaw-bone on both sides of her head was fractured, and she was otherwise mortally injured; in consequence of which injuries then and there wickedly and feloniously inflicted in manner above libelled, or in some other manner to the Prosecutor unknown, by you the said John Adam alias John Anderson, on the person of the said Jean [Jane] Brechin, she immediately or shortly thereafter died, and was thus murdered by you the said John Adam alias John Anderson; or you the said John Adam alias John Anderson did, by means of the aforesaid injuries, then and there wickedly and feloniously inflicted by you on the person of the said Jean [Jane] Brechin in manner above libelled, or in some manner to the Prosecutor unknown, and by means of throwing down upon her part of an old wall, consisting of turf and stones, and other materials, and covering her person therewith, and thus causing suffocation, or by some other means to the Prosecutor unknown, then and there, wickedly and feloniously put to death and murder the said Jean [Jane] Brechin: And that you the said John Adam alias John Anderson having been apprehended and taken before Alexander Mackenzie, Esquire, sheriff-substitute of Ross and Cromarty, you did, in his presence at Dingwall, on the

14th and 16th days of April 1835,

emit and subscribe two several declarations; and having been afterwards taken before *William Fraser Tytler, Esquire, Sheriff of the shire of Inverness, you did, in his presence at Inverness, on the*

7th day of May 1835,

emit and subscribe a declaration: Which declarations; as also a medical report or certificate, bearing to be dated on the 16th day of April 1835, and to be signed 'John Jones, Surgeon, William Hall, Surgeon'; as also a medical report or certificate, bearing to be dated on the 16th April 1835, and to be signed 'John Inglis Nicol, MD'; as also a map or plan, purporting to be a sketch of the site of, and ground about the house in which the dead body was found, and of a part of Ross-shire, bearing to be dated the 16th April 1835, and to be signed 'G Campbell Smith'; as also two stones; as also the various papers and articles specified in an Inventory hereunto annexed, being to be used in evidence against you the said John Adam alias John Anderson, at your trial, will, for that purpose, be in due time lodged in the hands of the clerk of the Circuit Court of Justiciary, before which you are to be tried, that you may have an opportunity of seeing the same: ALL WHICH, or part thereof, being found proven by the verdict of an Assize, or admitted by the judicial confession of you the said John Adam alias John Anderson, before the Lord Justice-General, Justice-Clerk and Lords Commissioners of Justiciary, in a circuit court of Justiciary to be holden by them, or by any one or more of their number, within the Burgh of Inverness, in the month of September, in the present year 1835, you the said John Adam alias John Anderson OUGHT to be punished with the pains of law, to deter others from committing the like crimes in all time coming.

Despite the belief of the Procurator-Fiscal and the Crown Officers that the date of the murder was Monday 30 March, it seems that it was decided to be wary and include the probability of dates up to Monday 6 April - thus reducing the possibility of John Adam providing an alibi. However, the inclusion of the possibility of the murder being committed in either February or May seems excessively cautious. It is also notable that the Crown authorities must not have been totally convinced that Jane's death had been caused by the blows to her head as conjectured in the doctors' reports. Thus they had included into the indictment the possibility of suffocation.

The annexed inventory contained a list of 52 articles referred to and libelled on in the indictment:

- 3 deposit receipts from the National and British Linen Banks;
- Articles of female clothing – 5 gowns, 4 petticoats, 3 shawls, 2 aprons, 2 bonnets, 2 caps, 2 pairs of shoes, 2 pairs of stockings, pair of stays, pair of gloves, a shift marked 'JB', a veil, a silk band, a mantle, a handkerchief;
- Other personal items – a woman's pocket, an umbrella, a gold marriage ring;
- Items of furniture and furnishings – mahogany chest of drawers, hardwood tent bed, a trunk, a square deal box, a clothes basket, a wicker reticule basket, 2 bed curtains, 4 bed covers, a cloth;
- Ornaments and other household items – pair of Derbyshire spar ornaments, pair of copper scales and balance, 3 tin scoops, glass sugar bowl, tin tea box, filler and measures.

All these items had been included in the lists contained in the package of documents sent by Hugh Cameron to David Cleghorn on Tuesday 11 August. However, other items had also been included in these lists, for example: cups, saucers, milk jug and other crockery; mattress, bolster and pillows; John's wedding clothes; and several items of table linen and female clothing, many marked 'JB'. It is not certain why they had been excluded from the inventory but, presumably, it was considered unlikely that reference would be made to them during the trial.

The list of witnesses annexed to the indictment contained 53 names. These were persons who had been precognosed and who were to be called to attend the trial [although the name of John Inglis Nicol MD appears twice, thus the list actually contained only 52 individuals]. They were:

- 7 law officers from Dingwall and Inverness;
- 3 surgeons from Dingwall and Inverness;
- 12 residents of the Black Isle;
- 9 residents of Dingwall;
- 10 residents of Montrose;
- 8 residents of Inverness;
- 1 carter from Elgin;
- 1 surveyor from Banff;
- Dorothy Elliott from Wirksworth.

Between Friday 4 September and Saturday 12 September these witnesses were summoned by the respective Sheriffs of Montrose, Inverness and Dingwall to attend the Circuit Court in Inverness on Friday 18 September 1835.

After receiving his copy of the indictment, John Adam appointed Charles Stewart, a senior partner of the firm of Stewart, Rule & Burns of Bank Lane, Inverness, as his defence solicitor. Their first meeting seems to have been on Wednesday 16 September, only two days before the trial. Next day Charles Stewart met with two advocates, James Crawford and Edward Gordon, who had been appointed as John's defence counsel. They prepared and issued John's defence[54]: *The pannel [the term used in Scots law for the accused person, ie John Adam] generally pleads not guilty. He denies the whole statements made in the libel and in particular he denies that upon either of the days libelled on as that on which the act is alleged to have been committed [Monday 30 March and Monday 6 April 1835], he was at or near the Heights or Braes of Kilcoy, but avers and offers to prove that he was engaged in his usual occupation near Dingwall. He offers to prove that he has borne a good character at Dingwall where he has resided for some time, and that his dispositions are quiet, peaceable and inoffensive.*

The improper and cruel publication of statements regarding the pannel, all of which are most positively denied, has tended to prejudice the public mind against him; and he earnestly trusts that on an occasion of such deep and momentous interest to him, the evidence may be carefully and impartially considered, and all such reports and statements will be disregarded by the jury.

The same day as John Adam's defence statement was released, Wednesday 16 September, the *Inverness Courier* carried a short article: *The Inverness Circuit Court opens here on Friday. There are 16 cases for trial. Adam, accused of the Millbuie murder, still denies his guilt, and conducts himself with indifference. We found him the other day playing at pitch-and-toss with the other prisoners in the passage used as an airing ground!*

After the customary parade of the High Court officials dressed in their finery through the streets of Inverness, John Adam's trial commenced at 10.00 am on Friday 18 September. The presiding judge was Advocate-Depute John Shaw-Stewart, Lord Moncrieff. The names of all jurors cited to attend were read out and several were fined for non-attendance [the statutory fine was £5]. Lord Moncrieff remarked that: *so many of the certificates of ill-health granted by medical gentlemen were informal and useless because they were not given upon 'soul and conscience'.*

The brief official minute[55] is the only formal record of the trial proceedings, however the press (particularly the *Inverness Courier*) were present and subsequent issues of local and national titles contained long and detailed accounts syndicated from this source. John was brought to the bar and the indictment was read. He was described as a tall handsome man, 31 years of age, well-dressed and very bald. He normally wore a wig but, on this occasion he did not, and consequently *had an older appearance than he normally presents.* In a firm tone, he pleaded *NOT GUILTY.*

A jury of the following 15 persons was appointed by ballot from the 65 persons named in the List of Assize[56] summoned to appear as special or common jurors. [Special jurors, who comprised one-third of the jury in a criminal trial, were persons who possessed land yielding £100 or more in annual rents or persons with over £1000 of personal property. The five special jurors for John Adam's trial are indicated by an asterisk in the list below.]

*Alexander Brander of Springfield, banker, Elgin
*Arthur Cant of Millfield, Nairn
*Capt William Fyfe, Garmouth, Elgin
Robert Grigor, merchant, Cromarty
James Hill, Cromarty
James Hoyes, farmer, Belnaferry, Elgin
Alexander MacCulloch, draper, Inverness
Donald MacLennan, factor, Glenelg, Inverness-shire
John McNicol, tacksman, Miltown of Kilravock, Nairn
*Hugh Munro, tacksman, Assynt, Ross-shire
*Col John Munro of Teaninich, Ross-shire
Alexander Rose, cartwright, Tomnarrach, Nairn
James Rose, farmer, Rearple, Nairn
Alexander Scott, farmer, Easter Manbeen of Pittendriech, Elgin
Thomas Turnbull, skinner, Inverness.

As soon as the jury was empanelled, John's 'special' defences were presented by his counsel, James Crawford. The Crown Counsel, Advocate-Depute David Cleghorn, then referred the jury to the indictment and the inventory of Jane Brechin's household goods and clothing detailed in the annex, before specifying the further exhibits that he intended to use in support of the case for the prosecution – the three bank deposit receipts[57] in favour of Jane Brechin and two stones with which he would contend the murder had been committed. He then commenced his case by confirming with Sheriff-Substitute Alexander Mackenzie, Procurator-Fiscal Hugh Cameron and Sheriff William Tytler that the three declarations made by John Adam had been *voluntarily emitted in his sober senses*. In his cross-examination, however, James Crawford pointed out that John Adam had been taken to view the body of the deceased on the day preceding his 1st declaration and questioned whether Hugh Cameron recalled asking John whether he believed in a God before subjecting him to the bier-right and afterwards declaring that they were all in the presence of God, who knew best. Hugh Cameron admitted that he had no recollection and James Crawford therefore objected that John's 1st declaration had later been taken *under the sanction of something of the nature of an oath*. In responding to this objection, David Cleghorn called John Macbean, the Messenger-at-Arms who had been present at the bier-right. He said that Hugh Cameron had used some expression to the effect that they were *standing in the presence of God* but could not recall whether the words were spoken before or after John Adam was asked to touch the corpse.

This potentially damaging (to the prosecution) objection to the 'admissibility' of John's declarations, however, was quickly repelled by Lord Moncrieff who ruled that the questions and remarks made at the bier-right had no bearing on the declarations and there was therefore *no foundation for the fact alleged in the objection.* [Lord Moncrieff was not actually correct on this point – the bier-right is described in John's 1st declaration – thus it is questionable whether this legal point should have resulted in John's acquittal. Clearly, Lord Moncrieff was not prepared to permit a technical flaw in the taking of a witness statement to de-rail the trial.]

Jane Stewart, Margaret (Peggy) Stewart and William Forbes, all of Muckernich, were called as witnesses to the discovery and initial unearthing of the corpse. Neither Jane nor Peggy could speak English, so Rev John Kennedy of Killearnan parish was sworn in as an interpreter of Gaelic. [In 1843, by which time he had become minister of Dingwall parish, Rev John Kennedy was to play a prominent role in the 'Disruption', during which the Free Church of Scotland was formed. He is commemorated by a large statue outside the Dingwall Free Church.] Then, George Campbell Smith of Banff, referring to his map, described the location of the old cottage where the corpse was found.

Drs John Jones and William Hall, who had carried out the on-site examination of the body and had performed the post-mortem, described the injuries to Jane's head - which corresponded with the shapes of the corners of two blood-stained stones that had been found by the body. These stones were exhibited to the Court, one being described as *an immense stone of about 28 pounds*. Both doctors had agreed at the time of writing their report that there was no evidence of suffocation and had ruled out any possibility that the stones had accidentally fallen on the body. They had also formed an initial opinion from the *fresh condition of the body* that it had lain for only 2-3 days but, later, had agreed that this may have been longer as the conditions under which the body had lain were *particularly favourable* to preservation and conducive to *retarding putrefaction* – of which there had been no sign.

In his cross-examination, counsel for the defence James Crawford attempted to create confusion in the minds of the jury on both the date and the manner of the death. John Jones was queried on whether he had changed his mind on the length of time the body had lain at the old cottage after, or before, he *had heard any circumstances of the case*. The doctor responded that he did not recall. It was also noted that William Hall had, after further reflection since the signing of the medical report, taken another view on the wounds to the head and the fractures of the jaw – now believing that they were insufficient to have caused instantaneous death as *he had attended persons with severer wounds, who had recovered rapidly*. James Crawford then reminded the jury that *the brain was charged with more dark-coloured blood than was natural, and the lungs were distended, which together were symptomatic of suffocation to a certain degree* – thus implanting the idea that Jane Brechin had perhaps not died solely of her head wounds. The credibility of the two doctors' report was further challenged by Dr John Inglis Nicol of Inverness who did not think that *there was anything in the circumstances attending the situation to accelerate or retard decomposition* and had concluded that the body must have been dead for 10-15 days when he saw it in Dingwall on Thursday 16 April.

The prosecution next turned to the identification of Jane Brechin's body, furniture and belongings by Margaret Munro and Archibald Gouk from Montrose; and by Janet and Hector MacIntosh from Inverness. The MacIntoshes also confirmed that the day of John and Jane's departure from Inverness was Friday 3 April 1835 and that Jane was carrying an umbrella and a reticule basket containing a pair of stockings, one of which was still wired and unfinished. Rev John Cook from Laurencekirk confirmed that he had married the couple at

Jane's mother's house on Wednesday 11 March.

Roderick MacGregor, the Kessock ferryman, and Robert Thomson, the carter from Charlestown, then confirmed the various crossings of the ferry by John Adam and the carting of Jane's furniture to Dingwall. Roderick also described the crossing, *on the Thursday or Friday after the furniture had been taken*, when John had been accompanied by a woman. He could not describe the woman's dress as it was dark and *Adam and the woman were sitting by each other at the stern of the boat; and he [Roderick MacGregor] was steering.* After landing, John and the woman had gone away together towards Dingwall and he had not seen either of them come back.

John, Christian and Jean Urquhart described how they had provided lodgings in Dingwall for John Anderson (Adam) and the woman of 18-22 years of age that they took to be his wife, Dorothy (Elliott). They also told of the occasions when John had departed for the south, claiming on one occasion to be visiting his brother and on the other to be collecting a legacy from an aunt, items of whose furniture had been carted to Dingwall. They were, however, somewhat vague about exactly which days John had visited Inverness but Christian remembered after one visit seeing some clothes and a basket that she had not seen before, as well as a pair of stockings, one of which was half-finished – and had subsequently been finished by Dorothy. Again attempting to create doubt about John's movements in the minds of the jury, James Crawford conjectured, somewhat sarcastically, that he thought these witnesses *would have missed John if he had gone away for a day.*

The final witnesses called by the Crown Counsel were Robert Gordon of the National Bank in Dingwall, James Beattie of the British Linen Bank in Montrose and David Hill of the National Bank in Montrose. They verified that Jane Brechin and John Anderson (Adam) had made the various cash deposits and withdrawals into and from their respective banks during 1834-35. James Beattie, however, could not positively identify John Adam as the person who withdrew £96, plus interest, from his branch on Monday 9 March 1835.

John Adam's three declarations[44] were then read to the jury. They were reported as having *caused a strong sensation in court,* after which David Cleghorn declared his evidence for the prosecution to be concluded – having called only 24 of the Crown's list of 52 witnesses named in the indictment. James Crawford then called his only witness *in exculpation of the Pannel [proving the innocence of the accused].* This was David Sutherland, the tenant of Craig Quarry, who described John Anderson as *a steady, industrious and sober man (who) was also harmless and inoffensive* and who, for some days previous to his apprehension, was *cheerful and good-humoured at work as usual and had shown no change in his demeanour.* However, David Sutherland's employment records[58] could not prove that John had worked on Friday 3 April as he always entered in his book *the first day of the month on which each man at the quarry is at work, and afterwards makes a score for each succeeding day in that month. The first entry made for John Anderson was on the 6th, so he was not at work before that day in April.* No further evidence was brought forward in support of John's plea of innocence.

David Cleghorn and James Crawford summed up respectively for the prosecution and defence. In the words of the *Inverness Courier* of Wednesday 23 September 1835: *He [David Cleghorn, Advocate-Depute] begged them [the jury] to dismiss from their minds all previous impressions they might have derived from the rumours that had gone abroad, and to confine themselves to the legal evidence that had been adduced. God forbid that he should seek to aggravate the case of the prisoner, charged with the highest crime known to the law, and committed under circumstances of deliberation, of cruelty, and of cold-blooded atrocity, that never had been surpassed, if they had been equalled in the annals of crime. The learned prosecutor then recapitulated the principal heads of the evidence. He remarked on the discrepancy between the evidence of the Urquharts at Dingwall, and that of the MacIntoshes in Inverness, as to the day on which the prisoner and his wife left their lodgings in Inverness. The testimony of the former went to prove that it was on Monday, and the latter distinctly specified Friday. The prisoner in his 3rd declaration stated Monday to be the day, and he (the public prosecutor) concurred in the*

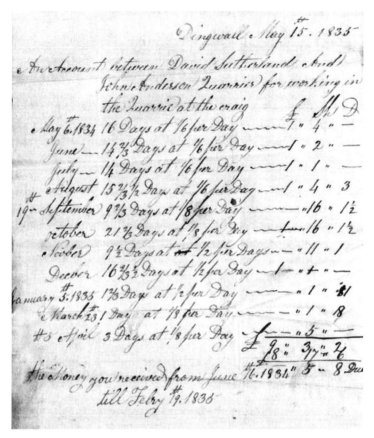

Figure 32: John Adam's employment record at Craig quarry from May 1834 to April 1835 (National Records of Scotland)

belief that this was the day on which the fatal deed was perpetrated. With the exception of this slight difference, the evidence was complete against the prisoner, and agreed in all its parts. The connection of the prisoner with the deceased – their marriage – their travelling together to Inverness – his conduct before and after the event – the fact that the deceased was last seen in life with the prisoner – the circumstances that the wearing apparel and effects of the deceased were, after the death, found in his house – all these points were readily established. After adverting to the contradictory nature of the prisoner's declarations, the learned gentleman concluded by expressing his conviction that there was sufficient evidence to prove that the deceased came by her death by the hand of the prisoner, and by none other.

James Crawford [Defence Counsel] addressed the jury for the prisoner. He commenced by entreating them to free their minds entirely of any prejudice, or suspicions which might have been created by the publications or rumours regarding this case, they were now within the hallowed precincts of a jury box– bound by a solemn oath to decide the case not only according to the evidence, but solely on the evidence laid before them. The more enormous and revolting was the crime of which the pannel was accused, just the more imperative was the obligation on the jury to estimate deliberately and rigidly the evidence on which they must decide his fate. In the case of treason, the accused party is fenced and surrounded by the most anxious and peculiar protection, and as no crime could be more cold blooded, premeditated and atrocious than that of which the prisoner is accused, so in no case could they be called on in the discharge of their duty to be more scrupulous and impartial in testing and estimating the evidence. [The reference to treason being the 'highest crime known in the land' was a piece of legal wit aimed at David Cleghorn who had, in his summing-up, described murder as 'the highest crime known to the law'.]

The prosecutor had rightly divided the case into two branches: the proof of the corpus delicti – did the woman die by violence? – and the connection of the prisoner with her death – was that violence inflicted by the hand of the prisoner? On both of these points he contended that the prosecutor's proof was defective. The possibility of the poor woman having been destroyed by the accidental falling of the wall was not excluded by the proof, and if not so excluded, if there was any ground for believing it possible that her death might have been caused in this manner, the jury were bound to give the prisoner the benefit of such a possibility. The medical men had indeed stated that the wounds were the cause of her death, but they had not sworn that these wounds had been inflicted during life, a circumstance of great importance and one which medical men are enabled with some degree of certainty to decide. They might have been inflicted after death, in the course of burying her in the rude way in which the body was covered, and the opinion of the medical men that the injuries caused death was thus formed on the assumption without proof that these injuries were inflicted during life. The proof of death by violence was thus defective. But the proof that, if she died by violence, it was inflicted by the pannel was still more objectionable. It was true there were circumstances of suspicion in the conduct of the prisoner, and particularly in his false declarations; but these were all to be accounted for on the supposition that he acted a deceitful and treacherous part towards the poor woman, in marrying her to obtain possession of her money and property and then deserting her – and did not necessarily or even fairly involve him in the guilt of murder. The opinions of the medical men differed materially as to the period of the woman's death, and the evidence as to the day of her leaving Inverness was altogether contradictory, the man MacIntosh and his wife fixing positively on Friday 3rd April, while the people at Dingwall prove that the prisoner was on that day at Dingwall, and although he was at Inverness on the Monday preceding, he was not proved to have seen the woman on that day at all. The prisoner was proved to have crossed the ferry, Thursday or Friday being the day fixed by the ferryman – but no proof was adduced that the woman ever crossed at all – she never was seen alive on the north side of the ferry. The previous character of the prisoner was proved to have been steady, quiet, gentle and inoffensive, and his remaining at Dingwall working as usual after the discovery of the body was quite inconsistent with the idea that he had been guilty of such a horrid murder. The Counsel concluded by urgently pressing on the jury the duty of weighing the evidence with great care, and of giving the pannel the benefit of any rational doubts they might entertain.

Lord Moncrieff [the Judge] summed-up at great length. The charge in the indictment, he said, was one of the foulest murders perpetrated in our day, and as regarded the prisoner one of the deepest die. He alluded to the obscurity in which all such cases were enveloped, as in *nine cases out of ten – he might say ninety in a hundred – murder was committed in such a way as no direct evidence could be found. His Lordship reviewed the different points in the evidence bearing against the prisoner, and also the contradictions contained in his declarations. It was in the prisoner's favour that he did not fly, though he had the money in his possession; he did not fly even when he heard that the body of the woman was brought to Dingwall. Nor did it appear that on the trying occasion of his being shown the body did he evince any agitation. His Lordship then went over the whole of the evidence, commenting on it with his usual ability and impartiality.*

The jury retired at 12.30 am on Saturday 19 September – 14½ hours after the trial had commenced. The official minute of the trial[55] records the process: *Lord Moncrieff charged the jury – and it being now half past twelve o'clock, his Lordship ordains the assize [jury] to inclose in a room adjoining, and to return their verdict in this place, as soon as they or a majority of them, are agreed therein, continues the diet against the pannel and ordains him to remain at the bar.*

During the retirement, John is said to have taken the opportunity to withdraw for a few minutes and, on his return, to have conversed with his counsel and others with utmost composure. The jury took 45 minutes to reach their verdict, so it has to be assumed that it was not an entirely clear-cut decision. Presumably, at least initially, some of the jury had been influenced by the totally circumstantial nature of the evidence, the confusion over the actual date of the murder or the discordant opinions of the doctors over the cause of the death.

The official minute of the trial continues: *The diet was again called at a quarter past one o'clock in the morning of 19 September and the jury returned into court and being called over and answering to their names, gave in the following viva voce verdict by the mouth of their Chancellor, Col John Munro. The jury unanimously find the pannel John Adam alias John Anderson GUILTY of the murder of Jane Brechin, as set forth in the indictment.*

Lord Moncrieff responded to the verdict at great length – reported in the *Inverness Courier* of Wednesday 23 September 1835: *Lord Moncrieff then put on the black cap and proceeded to pass sentence* to the prisoner. His Lordship was at times much affected, and the solemnity of his address, and the manner in which it was delivered, moved many of the audience even to tears. As nearly as we could follow the learned Judge, he spoke of this effect: John Adam (here the prisoner stood up in a firm, soldier-like manner) – unhappy and miserable man! After an anxious investigation, in the course of which every thing that could be done for your defence has been adopted, the jury has unanimously found you guilty: and it is my duty to say, that I cannot see how by any possibility they could have returned another verdict. It is but too plain, and all the history of the case discloses, that you have worked yourself up to a terrible state of mind. When you come to see things aright, all will appear light as air compared with the things of eternity. Going on from one sin to another –from one heartless crime to another – in a dark hour of your existence the Prince of Darkness took advantage of you, and in a bloody action, which, deep as are many of the cases that become before us, is almost unparalleled in enormity, has sealed your guilt. Having deceived one poor woman, bringing her away from her parents in sad reliance on the word of man, you practised on the feelings of another, and brought yourself into a condition in which secrecy would no longer avail you; then you consummated all by the awful crime of murder. No nation can do otherwise than punish this crime with death. It is condemned by the law of God as well as by the law of man, and in pronouncing that sentence now to be recorded against you, I am but the feeble instrument of justice. I know not whether I can say to you that this is a calamity. This will depend on the use you will make of the brief space of time still left you. If you had proceeded in that system of lies and crime which you have followed, sure I am, that unless you be still more deeply sunk in an infidel mind, and in disregard for the laws of God and man, than I think you are, you must have spent the most miserable life all the remainder of your days. I speak of this that I may earnestly beseech you to remember that there is yet a little time before your eyes will be shut on all things in this visible earth – before you die an ignominious death and stand before the judgement seat of God, with all your sins upon you, and this great crime as the *capital of all. Treat not this matter lightly; for as sure as the word of the eternal God, the same moment that severs your soul from your body will summon you before a righteous Judge. But there is a refuge for you and for the chief of sinners in the blood of Him who died for all, and who left it as his last legacy to mankind, so that even the malefactor who was with him on the cross, believing in the power of that atonement was saved. "This day," said He, "thou shalt be with me in Paradise." The words he addressed to him, he addresses to you, if you believe and repent. Listen to the exhortations brought you, and even at the eleventh hour you may be saved. Look only to the mercy and power of God for salvation. Do not occupy yourself in vain hopes that your sentence may be altered, or with the vain delusion that there is no reality in a hereafter. It is now full time that you forsake your refuges for lies. Believe me, I feel it to be painful to pronounce a sentence of death against a human being – I feel for your situation as deeply as any man can do. You have been tried by your fellow men under the sanction of their oaths, as they shall soon have to answer for to God; for we also are mortals and know not how soon we shall stand before the judgement seat of God – perhaps even before you. With these feelings of deep awe and commiseration I exhort you to prepare yourself for death. Apply to the Ministers of our holy religion in this place. Take the counsel they give you, and I trust there may yet be redemption for you.*

His Lordship then read the sentence, which was that the pannel, John Adam alias John Anderson, should be hanged at the usual place of execution in Inverness on Friday the 16th day of October next, between the hours of two and four o'clock in the afternoon, and his body afterwards buried within the precincts of the jail.

It seems that throughout the three closing speeches, John Adam had sat unmoved; and during the judge's pronouncement of the sentence he had silently stood to attention. After his sentence was passed, he had tried to address the jury – but the general commotion in the court had prevented him from being heard. Before being taken from the court, however, he is recorded as having called out: You have condemned an innocent man. *I have been condemned at the bar of man, but I will not be condemned at the bar of God.*

The full text of the sentence is recorded in the brief official minute of the trial[55]: *In respect of the foregoing verdict of assize the Lord Moncrieff decerns and adjudges the said John Adam, alias John Anderson, pannel, to be carried from the bar to the Tolbooth of Inverness therein to be detained until Friday the sixteenth day of October next to come; and upon that day, to be taken furth of the said Tolbooth, to the common place of execution of the Burgh of Inverness, or to such place as the Magistrates of Inverness shall appoint as a place of execution, and then and there betwixt the hours of two and four in the afternoon, to be hanged by the neck, upon a gibbet, by the hands of the Common Executioner, until he be dead, and ordains his body thereafter to be buried within the precincts of the said Tolbooth or prison of Inverness which is pronounced for Doom, and ordains all his moveable goods and gear to be escheat [confiscated] and inbrought to His Majesty's use; requiring hereby the Magistrates of Inverness and keepers of their Tolbooth, to see this sentence put in execution, as they shall be answerable at their highest peril.*

Editions of the *Inverness Courier* were published on Wednesdays and of the *Inverness Journal* on Fridays, so it was the *Inverness Courier* on Wednesday 23 September that had the first opportunity to provide the public with an account of the trial. This it did at great length, consuming almost the whole of the back page with extensive details of the event. In contrast, the *Inverness Journal* [which had 'scooped' the discovery of the murdered body in its edition of Friday 10 April] published only a brief paragraph on Friday 25 September. However, this paragraph was the first to introduce the Rev Alexander Clark, the minister of Inverness parish church, who was to feature significantly in the post-trial events: *Thereafter [after the preliminaries] John Adam or Anderson was brought to the bar, indicted for the murder of Jane Brechin, his wife. The particulars of this long trial would occupy five or six columns, and as there is nothing in it materially different from what has been already before the public, the same universal conviction of the prisoner's guilt being common to the jury, and to the public, we shall not repeat the statements which have been already before them.*

His own details were in many instances very contradictory of his assertions on former examinations, as often happens from the lapse of memory, and the attempts of conscious guilt, to escape punishment. After his condemnation he sent for Rev Mr Clark, who has seen him several times since. In his presence he is often affected to tears, but he has not yet confessed. Mr Clark thinks he will: the impression which their several conversations have left on his mind being, that there is no doubt of his guilt.

Unsurprisingly, the newspapers that had carried articles on the discovery of the murder and the subsequent events also published full accounts of the trial – the *Arbroath, Montrose & Brechin Review* on Friday 25 September, the *Caledonian Mercury* on Saturday 26 September and *The Times* on Wednesday 30 September. The former two titles used more or less the full account of the trial syndicated by the *Inverness Courier*. However, *The Times* chose only to precede the *Inverness Courier's* account of Lord Moncrieff's pronouncement of the sentence with a brief apology: *After a lengthened trial, which we are sorry the press of matter connected with our own Circuit Court prevents us from giving, the jury returned an unanimous verdict, finding the prisoner GUILTY, as set out in the indictment.*

The costs of John Adam's trial mostly fell on the Circuit Court of Justiciary. However, some incidentals appear in an entry in the Inverness Burgh Treasurer's accounts[59] for 1835-36 under the heading of 'Expenses of Circuit Court'. This shows expenditure for a coach and 4 horses to transport the judges (£1-4/-), refreshments (£1-8-6d), stationery (£2-19/-) and a scarlet cloth (4/-), totalling £5-15-6d.

CHAPTER EIGHT

Execution

Immediately after the trial, the magistrates of Inverness received a death warrant[60] containing instructions from Lord Moncrieff to make arrangements for an execution. It was to be performed on Friday 16 October by the Common Executioner at a gibbet to be erected at a location appointed by them.

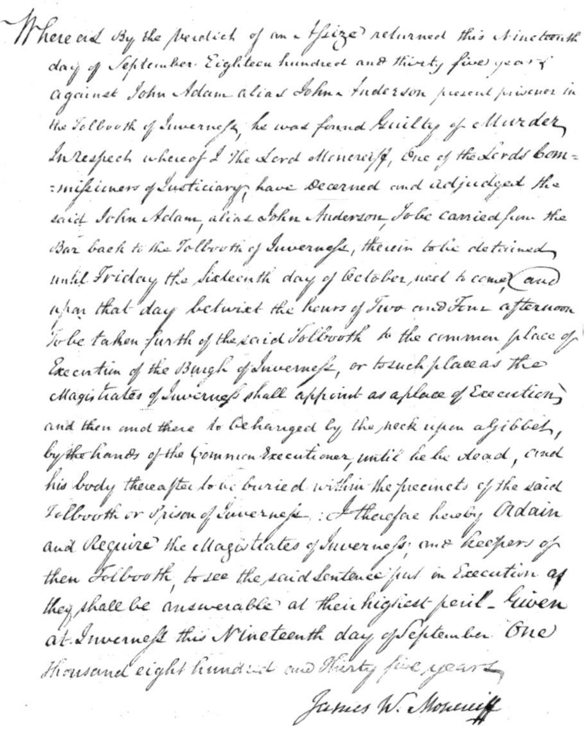

Figure 33: John Adam's execution warrant issued by Lord Moncrieff on 19 September 1835 (reproduced with permission of the Highland Archive Service)

Scottish municipalities were reformed in 1833 when direct elections to Royal and Parliamentary Burgh Councils were introduced. One of the first decisions of the newly elected Inverness Town Council had been to abolish, on 19 December 1833, the post of the Burgh hangman, Donald Ross. He was said to have performed only three executions throughout the entire 21 years of his appointment since 1812, although only two are recorded to have taken place in Inverness[61] – those of Robert Ferguson on 13 November 1812 and Hugh McLeod, the 'Assynt Murderer', on 24 October 1831. Robert Ferguson had been the last person to be hanged at the Barron Muir, close to the Edinburgh Road, where a permanent gibbet had stood since at least 1750. [This gibbet is illustrated on John Home's 1774 plan of the River Ness[62] and on Taylor & Skinner's 1776 road map[50].] Hugh McLeod had been hanged at the Longman, near the shore of the Moray Firth, where there was more viewing space and where Donald Ross had constructed a gibbet especially for the event. For his part in these executions he had received substantial remuneration, including a house, bedding, fuel, food and clothing – valued at approximately £60 per year, a generous salary in the early-19th century.

An interesting (although suspect) account of Donald Ross and his role as hangman can be found in Joseph Mitchell's *Reminiscences of my Life in the Highlands* published in two volumes in 1883-4. He recalls that Donald Ross was a condemned sheep-stealer who was pardoned on condition that he agreed to become the Burgh hangman. He proceeds to state that the office was no sinecure, *as there was generally a hanging at every circuit in April and August* and there were *loose women condemned by the magistrates to be whipped by the hangman.* This may have been the case in the 18th century when many offences attracted severe or capital punishment but not in the memory of Joseph Mitchell who was born in 1803. He concludes with the statement that *the last hangman [Donald Ross] has long since gone to his account. No successor was appointed or has been needed.*

Joseph Mitchell may not have recalled the case of John Adam when he made that statement, but the lack of a successor to Donald Ross meant that the magistrates of the town had no 'Common Executioner' to construct a gibbet and undertake an execution. However, a man named John Murdoch was quick to contact the Burgh officials to make an offer to perform the task of 'turning off' John Adam. As most Burghs had dispensed with their hangman by 1835, John Murdoch, who originated from Glasgow, had become a follower of the Circuit Courts around Scotland looking for opportunities to ply his trade. He was appointed to perform the task. [*'Turning him off'* was a Scots slang term for an execution by hanging. It referred to the old practice of making the condemned man climb a ladder with the noose around his neck and falling when the hangman turned the ladder.]

At the conclusion of his trial, John Adam was returned to his cell in Inverness Tolbooth. There is said to have been an incident before the trial when a razor had been discovered in his clothes. Fearing that there was a possibility of him attempting to commit suicide, he had been fettered in chains and two guards had been placed inside his cell. He had protested at this precaution, claiming that it inferred *an unjust suspicion against him* and complaining that he could not get regular sleep due to his guards keeping a candle alight during the night. Otherwise, John is said to have talked congenially with his jailors about his adventures in the Army and to have confessed many past sins – especially his conduct towards Dorothy Elliott and Jane Brechin, the two women he had betrayed, and the other cases of seduction that he had committed. However, in discussing the murder, he had maintained a cool indifference, always asserting his innocence although acknowledging that nobody believed him.

As had previously been noted in articles published by the *Inverness Journal* on Friday 29 May and the *Inverness Courier* on Wednesday 1 July, John had increasingly taken solace in reading the Bible during his imprisonment. Immediately after the trial, perhaps showing that he had paid attention to Lord Moncrieff's address from the bench, John had requested an audience with Rev Alexander Clark. The minister had readily acceded to this request as he had been anxious to get John to confess his guilt and repent, believing by doing so, John would receive Christian redemption and escape consignment to eternal suffering in Hell. However, Rev Clark had been unsuccessful. In what seems to have been an 'energetic' meeting, Rev Clark had stated with some force that he had studied the evidence carefully and *had not the shadow of doubt that he was addressing a murderer of the deepest dye*; whilst John, for his part, had been equally resolute in denying his guilt. Despite their differences of opinion, however, the two men seem to have departed on friendly terms and, during the few remaining weeks before the execution, they held regular conversations. Other ministers also went to the Tolbooth on occasions, but all failed to elicit a confession.

Rev Alexander Clark was a native of Inverness who had been educated at the Inverness Royal Academy and who had graduated in 1813 from King's College, Aberdeen. He had returned to Inverness in 1834 to take up his post as Inverness parish minister based at the Old High Church, which stands on St Michael's Mound overlooking the River Ness. The present building dates mainly from 1772 but the site has been an important religious centre ever since St Columba preached to King Brude there in the 6th century.

Another person who seems to have visited and befriended John was Ebenezer Davidson, the head teacher of Raining's School in Inverness. [This school was built in 1757 from an endowment of £1,200 by John Raining, a merchant from Norwich. It closed in 1894 when its pupils transferred to the nearby Inverness High School.] It is not clear how they first met (perhaps he had accompanied Rev Clark on a visit) but it appears that during one of their meetings John had mentioned the dream in which his fiancée had stood at the foot of his bed and had spoken the words: *John, we shall never be married – but mark, you will die an awful death*. The version told on this occasion seems to have been a little embellished – the girl had come to his bedside in the shape of a beautiful dove and had said: *John, we are not to be married; my time in this world will be very short. You are to die an awful death; but you and I shall be happy in the world to come.* Taken aback at John's reference to a happy afterlife, the headmaster had admonished John for putting his faith in dreams and had advised him to seek *a more solid means of reliance in the oracles of truth, and through the blood of atonement*.

John, however, was in no frame of mind to confess. He had been denied the opportunity to speak after the trial, so he set about writing down his version of the proceedings – anxious that it should be known before his execution because he feared he might be disinclined to make an address from the gallows or, if he did, might once again be unable to make himself heard. It is clumsily entitled 'A Sketch of the Trial of John Adam, who was tried at the last Circuit Court of Justiciary, held at Inverness, upon the 18th of September last' and was first published on Wednesday 14 October in the *Inverness Courier*. Despite being prefixed by the somewhat condescending statement: *We have made a few trifling corrections in the orthography but the unfortunate man both reads and writes tolerably well* – it is a decidedly rambling and disjointed account of his innocence and what he claims to have been deficiencies in his trial: *A number of witnesses examined at the trial were found to be much against me, although several of them could favour me were justice given. Two of the witnesses, in particular, who identified me as the person seen with the woman the day we left Inverness, to cross the ferry, on the way to Dingwall, I can solemnly say swore false oaths, which, if justice had been done, would have been in my favour; likewise, the medical men who examined the body of the woman, were confused in their opinions as to the time the body was dead; there was a difference of from no less than from 24 hours to 15 days. This, they said, was owing to evidence which, it seems, was in their opinion satisfactory. I am sensible, so many differences of opinions betwixt the witnesses examined against me, and the medical gentlemen who examined the body, and the false oaths (as I am certain in my own mind there was) show that I was unjustly dealt with in court, as to my mind, and I am certain that nothing but strong suspicion and false oaths were the cause of my condemnation for the crime above mentioned. I, therefore, solemnly warn jurymen sitting in judgement upon any trial, where a man's life is in their hands, to be more clear with regard to the witnesses, and see that no false oaths be allowed, as was in my case, merely because I was strongly suspected of the crime. Even the person who took us across the ferry could not give his oath as to that woman being the person found dead. All these serve, and leave room to the public at large to see, that nothing* but suspicion was at my trial; no clear evident proof that I was the person who committed the deed, and it is surely hard for a man to die for a crime merely because they were suspicious of him. Likewise false oaths being sworn against me, will open the eyes of the world; and surely there must be a remorse of conscience in those individuals who swore false oaths against me, and the medical gentlemen who passed their opinions upon the words of these persons; and also those jury men who passed the sentence, and found me guilty – it ought to be a solemn warning to them all, to be more clear and more just in their minds to those unfortunate persons whom crime, or being a companion to those who are guilty of crime, may bring before them for judgement. We have it recorded in scripture, that no man ought to condemn his fellow creature falsely, or take a false oath in his mouth against him, for God says, he that will do so must suffer, and that most justly. If many of my witnesses had been attentive in the perusal of their Bible, they would not have sworn falsely against me in a public court, when they were fully aware they were condemning themselves, as well as the unfortunate person before them, and for which they must be assured they will at some period or other be accountable. This is what makes me feel more wretched in my mind, when I see the way I have been dealt with at my trial. Even my Lord Moncrieff might have seen the stagnation of speech in the evidence of the ferry man which should have served to vindicate [convince] his Lordship that there was a something that ought to have been taken into consideration, and that all was not right in that man's proof against me. But it seems to me, as if the court determined to condemn me because they were suspicious of me. If the woman who swore with respect to my marriage was found to mistake in her evidence against me, with regard to the time of marriage, this and all other things might have served to vindicate [convince] the court of falsity. Indeed, most of the witnesses who were summoned to appear at my trial were found to differ in their evidence against me – this might serve to open the minds of those jury men. I solemnly say that the woman of whose death I am accused, that I departed with that woman at the windmill, this side of the ferry, and never saw that woman more till I saw her body in Dingwall jail. Of this I am positive, and can solemnly swear to the truth of. When I was taken up, and taken to Dingwall jail, the court must be aware of the hard usage upon me, at the sight of the corpse of the murdered person. If there was any feeling heart, that was a suitable time for doing so, but it seems that they determined to condemn me without being heard at all. But my witnesses who were so anxious for my condemnation, will feel a remorse of conscience for their falsity in condemning me. It was proved by the people whose house I lodged in, in Dingwall, that my landlady saw me take my dinner in my own house in Dingwall, that day at four o'clock, and saw me that night at eight o'clock, when it was falsely sworn by the person or persons who said I took my dinner in their house at Inverness, at four o'clock that same night, which was a most notorious falsehood, as the inmates of the house that I stopped in, in Dingwall, positively swore that I was at Dingwall that very day, on which I was supposed to be in Inverness. This might serve to vindicate [convince] the court that I am innocently condemned to die, for a crime of which I am not guilty. My trial proves that great falsity has been going on all along, but they must remember the consequences of all this, who have been the sole cause of my condemnation. I, therefore, blame them for it. Some of them knew well that what they said was false against me, and the jury men are much to blame in hearkening unto the evidence of a false witness; likewise, in condemning me merely upon a suspicion, for it was nothing else but suspicion that was at my trial. They ought most solemnly to have taken this seriously into their consideration, before they returned their verdict of guilty. Even the medical gentlemen who inspected the dead body could not give a decided opinion as to when the deed was committed, nor were they right in their opinions as to the time the body lay there, till false evidence was procured against me. I therefore feel in my own mind that I ought to say something for myself, that may give insight to the public of the unjust way that I have been dealt with at my trial, that they may judge the falsity of most of the witnesses who were examined against me. I solemnly say, that this should, and ought to be, a warning to those gentlemen who are appointed to sit as jury men in any court, that they ought to consider well their hearts, and they *ought to scrutinize well the witnesses before them, with regard to what they have to say, to see that it proceed[s] from a pure conscience; for many a witness may be regardless of what he says, as his conscience, perhaps even if he was swearing falsely, would not put him in the least afraid of what he said. How many cases of false evidence have been found in court, and many an unfortunate person punished, which the public afterwards, perhaps years after found out to be innocent. All these things ought to be seriously considered, for nothing can be worse than innocent condemnation in the sight of God – as we have it from scripture. Nothing can be more awful.*

Unfortunately John's 'sketch' failed to bring any new evidence or new interpretations that had not been brought out at the trial. His main contentions were those that his counsel had raised in his defence statement and in his cross-examinations during the trial: that the jury had a predetermined suspicion of his guilt that had prevented them from properly scrutinising the evidence; that some witnesses had made false statements; that the ferryman could not identify Jane as being the person with whom he had crossed the Kessock ferry; that Dingwall witnesses had proven that he was in Dingwall on the day he and Jane had supposedly left Inverness; and that the doctors had disagreed on the period of time that the body had lain undiscovered. John expressed this last point in an interesting way when he wrote: *nor were they right in their opinions as to the time the body lay.* Some observers have taken this statement as an admission of his guilt because only the murderer could have known that the doctors had wrongly stated how long the body had lain in the ruined cottage.

After writing his 'sketch', John is said to have received a long letter from his brother James, who had taken over the tenancy of the farm at Craigieloch. Both of his brothers [James and William] are said to have visited him in the Inverness Tolbooth and to have attended the trial – although there is no mention of this in any of the press reports. The letter urged John to confess his guilt and prepare himself for his inevitable death, but John's reply seems to have re-iterated much of his 'sketch', strongly denying his role in the crime. Throughout the six-month period since his arrest in April 1835, this brief exchange of letters (and unconfirmed attendance at the trial) seems to have been the only contact made between John and any of his family in Lintrathen.

On Wednesday 14 October, two days before the execution, John wrote a letter to Dorothy Elliott. It is said to have been written in affectionate terms and partly in his blood. On the next evening Dorothy visited John in his cell accompanied by one of the ministers, probably Rev Clark. It was a tearful and heart-rending meeting during which John repeatedly declared his innocence despite Dorothy's implorations to him to make a confession. According to one source, Dorothy's appeals were made so eloquently that they *might have melted a heart of stone – but his [John's] was made of iron*. In great distress, after bidding John her final farewell, Dorothy took her leave. John then turned to Rev Clark to make a request that perhaps revealed some of his true fondness towards Dorothy and even a veiled confession – *Oh, tell her to beware of bad company*.

As had been decreed by Lord Moncrieff, the execution took place on Friday 16 October 1835. The *Inverness Journal* carried a surprisingly brief article in its edition of that day but a much more detailed account was published by the *Inverness Courier* on Wednesday 21 October. After an introductory paragraph describing the anxious labours of the clergy to obtain a confession and noting that John had slept soundly the night previous to his death, the proceedings of the day are described in much lurid detail: *His fetters being struck off, the culprit washed and dressed himself in a long camlet black coat provided for the occasion. [Camlet was a cloth originally made from camel's hair but John's coat was probably of goat's hair.] He partook of a hearty breakfast. About one o'clock he was brought into the Court House (which communicates with the jail), his hands and wrists being pinioned. The Rev Messieurs Clark, Scott and Kennedy, the Provost and Magistrates, and a few other persons were present. Adam seemed pale from his long confinement, but in good health. [Actually, John had not been in good health in the later part of his confinement; there is an entry for 6/3d in the Burgh jail accounts for a visit to him on 1 August 1835 by Dr J Inglis Nicol – 3/6d for the visit and 2/9d for prescribed medicines.] Mr Scott then delivered an appropriate and* affecting prayer, after which Mr Clark gave out the two first verses of the 32nd psalm [Blessed is he whose transgression is forgiven], which were sung with much solemnity. Mr Kennedy delivered a prayer and the party quitted the Court House for the place of execution. Adam thanked Mr Fraser, the jailor, and the turnkey, who had been unceasing in their humane endeavours to soften the horrors of the prisoner's situation, which seemed to be felt by all but himself. Three carriages were drawn up in front of the jail, as it was feared the culprit and the executioner would not be able to forge their way through the dense mass of persons which thronged the streets, and in one of these was Adam accompanied by Mr Clark, Mr Kennedy and Mr E Davidson, schoolmaster, who had been very attentive to the prisoner during his confinement. [There were also two constables in John's carriage.] Adam was desirous of walking to the place of execution. He said he did not like to be driven to the gallows and hung up like a dog. On being informed, however, of the crowd collected on the streets, and the difficulty there would be in his walking to the place, he instantly assented to the arrangement. The other carriages were the Provost, Magistrates, Town Clerk, &c. Special constables were sworn in for the occasion, whose judicious exertions preserved the utmost order throughout the day. [200 constables were said to be on duty, of which 110 had been sworn in for the day.]

The place of execution at the Longman, on the eastern shore of the Moray Firth, is fully a mile from the town, and the whole of the road and fields were filled with individuals hurrying to the spot where the gallows was erected. At the last execution here in 1831, it was calculated that about eight thousand persons were present. The number on this occasion was even greater, and the effect of the whole scene was indescribably striking and impressive. On alighting from the carriage, Adam walked with a firm step up to the scaffold. He stole a glance at the vast crowd before him, but was calm and unmoved. His tall and handsome person, and respectable appearance, were the subject of universal remark. Several portions of Scripture suited to the occasion were read by Mr Clark, and prayers were said by the same gentleman and by Mr Kennedy. The latter had reference to the *impenitence of the culprit, but he heard them apparently without emotion. [John had previously requested Ebenezer Davidson to select a psalm to be read on the scaffold. He had suggested the 51st but John had thought the 31st to be more suitable – "a fearful proof of the still unsubdued state of his mind" – according to Ebenezer Davidson.]*

The executioner proceeded to make the necessary preparations; and Adam, being privately addressed by Mr Clark, requested that he might be remembered to his mother and friends. He again asseverated his innocence of the crime for which he was about to suffer, and said he was not afraid to meet God on the ground of his innocence! This declaration was heard with horror by the gentlemen near to him, who were well assured of his guilt. The unfortunate man in a few moments dropt a white handkerchief from his hand, as a signal to the executioner, and the drop fell. He struggled for some minutes, but not violently. The crowd beheld this awful scene without any expression of sympathy or regret, as was manifested at the execution of Macleod. A feeling of astonishment at the firmness of the criminal and at the hardihood of the assertions of his innocence, seemed to be the prevailing sentiment among all present. After hanging about an hour, the body was cut down, placed in a coffin, and re-conveyed to the jail. It has since been interred, as enjoined by the statute "within the precincts of the prison", a part of the pavement being taken up and a grave dug in the passage leading from the private door of the Court house to the jury room and bench. It is perhaps to be wished that this part of the Act of Parliament was omitted, as in many of the jails, particularly in Scotland, there are no airing-grounds which can be used for the purpose, and there is something offensive as well as unwholesome in converting the interior of a prison or Court room into a charnel-house for dead malefactors.

It is noteworthy that a description of the execution written many years later in 1883 in *Reminiscences of my Life in the Highlands* by Joseph Mitchell is at considerable variance with that provided by the *Inverness Courier*. Mitchell describes the event as follows: *The execution was conducted with great solemnity. The gallows was erected at the Longman ... round the gallows, twelve feet from the ground, was a raised platform on which the clergy and magistrates stood, the culprit on the drop. According to my recollection, the procession between the jail and the place of execution was very dreadful ... first came the town's officers with their red coats and halberds [combined axe and spear]; then the magistrates and the council. The culprit followed, attended by either one or two clergymen. He was clothed in a white robe, with bare neck, over which the noose of the rope hung loose, the upper end being borne by the hangman, who walked behind.* Joseph Mitchell never actually states that the execution he recalled was that of John Adam in 1835, so it may have been that of Hugh Macleod in 1831 (the only other execution to take place whilst Mitchell was in Inverness). If it was that of John Adam, it can only be surmised that he exercised imaginative licence in compiling his reminiscences.

The *Inverness Courier* article of Wednesday 21 October concludes that John Adam, untouched by remorse and unconscious of the awfulness of his situation, seems to have deluded himself that life was *no more than a dramatic scene, in which the actor should preserve his consistency to the last; and that, as he lived without virtue, he should die without repentance.* Rev Alexander Clark also contended that John Adam was delusional – in believing, firstly, that death was *a mere passing into nothingness, and had no terrors except a passing spasm of physical pain* and, secondly, that his sentence *was only a threat in order to extort a confession.* In respect of this latter contention, John seemed to think that his predecessor on the scaffold at the Longman, Hugh Macleod, like himself, had been convicted on purely circumstantial evidence and would not have been hanged if he had not confessed. Thus it has to be postulated that John Adam believed, right up to his fatal drop, that he would be reprieved.

The *Inverness Journal* and *Inverness Courier* articles of Friday 16 October and Wednesday 21 October respectively were picked up by many of the country's local and national newspapers and reproduced in varying haste, partially or in their entirety. On Tuesday 20 October, *The Times* dedicated only nine lines in its 'News in Brief' section. On Thursday 22 October, the *Caledonian Mercury* reproduced more or less the whole *Inverness Journal* article and the *Edinburgh*

Evening Courant carried a brief synopsis. On Friday 23 October, the *Arbroath, Montrose & Brechin Review* devoted considerable space to the account of the execution from the *Inverness Journal* and a verbatim reproduction of John Adam's 'sketch' from the *Inverness Courier* of Wednesday 14 October. On Saturday 24 October, the *Caledonian Mercury* followed up its previous article on the execution with a column entitled 'Adam the Murderer' taken from the portion of the *Inverness Courier* article that described the life of John Adam prior to the trial. On Friday 30 October, the *Arbroath, Montrose & Brechin Review* reproduced the entire *Inverness Courier* article. Several English newspapers also carried descriptions of the execution taken from the *Inverness Courier*, for example: the *Morning Post* (London) on Tuesday 20 October; the *Westmorland Gazette* and the *Leicester Chronicle* on Saturday 7 November; and the *Hereford Journal* on Wednesday 23 December 1835.

Remarkably, news of the execution also crossed the Atlantic Ocean to Newfoundland [many Inverness émigrés had settled there during and after the Highland clearances] where an article entitled 'Execution of John Adam, Inverness' featured in the Christmas Day 1835 edition of the *Public Ledger & Newfoundland General Advertiser*. The article was based on the *Inverness Courier* article of Wednesday 21 October 1835.

Responsibility for the execution had been given to George Cameron, the Inverness Burgh Chamberlain, and Alexander Grant, the Burgh Officer appointed to organise the event. They must have been satisfied with the efficiency with which John Murdoch, the executioner, had performed his task because the Inverness Burgh Treasurer's accounts[63] show that only three days after the execution he received payment of £35-17-10d in settlement of his fee and incidental expenses. Some of the invoices and receipts still survive in the Inverness Jail accounts[64] and give some insight into the details of the event. For example, it appears that 'Murdoch the Executioner' [the term used to identify John Murdoch in the accounts] was accommodated from Wednesday 23 September in the Tolbooth. He was provided with crockery and two 'Scotch blankets' [supplied by J. Clark's Woollen Manufactory] which were purchased for him by William Fraser, the head jailor, at a cost of 2/5½d and £1-3/- respectively. He also received 7/- per week for 'aliment' [food]. Thus, making allowance for other expenses such as travel, for which claims or receipts have not survived, it can be estimated that John Murdoch's fee was approximately £30-32, or perhaps 30 guineas.

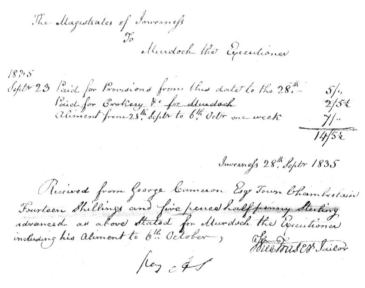

Figure 34: Receipted invoice from the Head Jailor to the Magistrates of Inverness for some of 'Murdoch the Executioner's' expenses (reproduced with permission of the Highland Archive Service)

These were by no means the only costs that fell on the magistrates of Inverness Burgh. It was customary at the time for all costs of detaining a criminal in prison up to the time of sentencing to be chargeable to the Exchequer. However, the expense of executing a condemned prisoner fell on the magistrates of the Burgh in which the execution was ordained to take place. As well as the fees and expenses of the executioner, these would have included costs associated with the prisoner's maintenance, transportation, burial, etc. and the process costs such as the payment of additional constables. Interestingly, the Provost of Inverness, John Mackenzie, had written on 24 March 1834 to the Lord Advocate on this matter. His long letter was published in the *Inverness Courier* on 26 March 1834. His main point was that *the hardship and injustice of the expense of capital punishments falling on a Burgh, is perhaps more glaring in this [Inverness] than in any other division of Scotland, as the town bears so very small a proportion in every point of view to the extent of country included within the Circuit bounds. This town contains only about 10,000 persons, while parties are tried here for crimes committed in the seven counties of Caithness, Sutherland, Ross, Cromarty, Inverness, Nairn and Moray, and in the several burghs and towns in these counties, being more than a third of the surface of Scotland.*

The letter proceeds to propose that *if the condemned criminals are to be all executed here, the expense ought to be borne either by the public at large or by the county or burgh in which the crime was committed. Or might it not be advisable to send the criminals, for the sake of example, to be executed where the crimes were committed, at the expense of the public or of such county or burgh, or to transfer criminals capitally convicted to the national gaol of Scotland for execution at Edinburgh.*

Provost Mackenzie then quotes some data to back up his case: *Inverness may fairly complain of the practice in question, as I cannot find a case on record of a capital punishment having been inflicted here for a crime committed within the burgh itself. Within the last fifty years, there have been eleven individuals sentenced at the Inverness Circuit Court to death, of whom only five were executed, viz – one sent from Ross-shire, one from Sutherland, one from Caithness, one from Moray, and one from Inverness – the last mentioned being the case of an Irishman, a soldier, for murder at Fort George. And the expense to Inverness during that period has been about £2,500! I am the more anxious to bring this matter under your Lordship's consideration at this time, because a case of murder committed in the county of Moray is to come before the Circuit Court to be held here on the 5th of May next; and if condemnation follows and the execution be ordered to take place in this burgh, we shall be subjected to very serious expense, as we have no executioner.*

Provost Mackenzie's plea fell on deaf ears. Although Inverness was spared the expense of hanging the Irishman [in May 1834 William Noble was the last person to be executed in Elgin], the Burgh did have to meet the cost of hanging John Adam one year later, in 1835. He was, however, the last person to be publicly hanged in Inverness.

It is likely that the execution of John Adam was John Murdoch's first appointment. Subsequently, he performed several more executions around Scotland until he retired in October 1851, at the age of 84, having made a shambles of his final execution in Glasgow – that of Archibald Hare. For that execution he had failed to make the drop sufficiently high and had to pull on Hare's legs to kill him. After John Murdoch's retirement, William Calcraft was appointed to undertake hangings in Scotland as general executioner for Great Britain.

The Treasurer's accounts[63] also identify three other execution costs: some incidental expenses incurred by Alexander Grant (6/3d); payments to the 'Post Boys' who drove the carriages to the Longman (9/-); and the expense of constructing the gallows (£3). [It is not stated whether John Murdoch built the gallows or sub-contracted it.] In combination, all of these items total £39-13-1d – the amount that is identified in the Burgh Chamberlain's discharge within the 1835-36 Burgh Treasurer's accounts for the execution of John Adam.

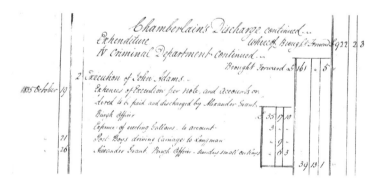

Figure 35: Inverness Town Chamberlain's accounts for 1835 showing the cost of John Adam's execution (reproduced with permission of the Highland Archive Service)

CHAPTER NINE

Postscripts and Revelations

(i) The Sermon

In the evening of the day of the execution, Rev Alexander Clark held a service in Inverness parish church during which he preached a sermon entitled 'God righteously abandoning Man'. The congregation was large, many being there in the expectation that Rev Clark would make a statement to the effect that John had ultimately confessed on the scaffold. There was, of course, no such announcement. The sermon, themed around a text taken from Psalm 81, verse 12 – *So I gave them up unto their own hearts' lust, and they walked in their own counsels* – was essentially a warning on the destiny that befalls those who are tempted, in the words of Rev Clark, *to plunge heedless into the current of powerful and dangerous sin.*

His opening words were dramatic: *I have been led to call your attention to this terrible subject, from the mournful scene which we witnessed this day. Never shall I forget the awful impression made upon my mind, on seeing an immortal spirit in a state of appalling religious insensibility, hurried into the presence of God, with numerous sins upon his head, as well as one awful crime ... he died as he lived, unrepenting and unforgiven ... surely there is nothing more solemnly awful than the death of a man abandoned by God.* Rev Clark then proceeded to give a lengthy account of John Adam's *life of uncommon sin, concluded by a crime of extraordinary atrocity, and a hopeless and miserable death*, before concluding: *I now solemnly commend you all, earnestly praying, that you may learn celestial wisdom from all the instructions of His word, and all the dispensations of His Providence, and more especially from the dismaying scene you witnessed this day. Amen!*

In its article describing the execution, the *Inverness Journal* of Friday 16 October 1835 refers to the Rev Clark's evening service, surmising (because it had not have been given at the time the newspaper was published) that the sermon was *preached on the melancholy occurrence of the day to a very crowded audience*. It was also noted that Rev Clark intended to publish the sermon and *as we shall give extracts from it in this Journal, we think it unnecessary to be more minute at present.*

Surprisingly, the *Inverness Courier* of Wednesday 21 October does not mention the evening service. However, the promised publication appeared in the *Inverness Courier* on Wednesday 20 January 1836 – three months after the sermon had been delivered. The reason for the delay was that Rev Clark had discovered some significant new information.

Before his execution, after he had dressed himself in the l*ong camlet black coat provided for the occasion*, John had left his clothes in the corner of his cell with directions that his jailors should give them to a fellow prisoner named John Sutherland, who was serving a six-month sentence for housebreaking and theft[65], and with whom he had become intimately friendly. When the clothes were handed over as instructed, John Sutherland revealed that John Adam had confidentially told him the full story of the murder – a story that John Adam had made him promise would not be recanted until after the execution. It is thought that John Sutherland subsequently committed the story to writing and gave the account to Rev Clark.

Thus, in possession of the revelations of John Sutherland, Rev Clark was able to incorporate them into the written version of his sermon that he had promised to publish. No copy of this publication appears to have survived but it was advertised as a pamphlet, priced 10d, on the front page of the *Inverness Courier* on Wednesday 20 January 1836 and the Inverness Journal on Friday 22 January 1836. The advertisement claimed that it contained *a full account of this savage murder and of the several particulars connected with it, as well as of the former life, crimes, impenitence and execution of the murderer.*

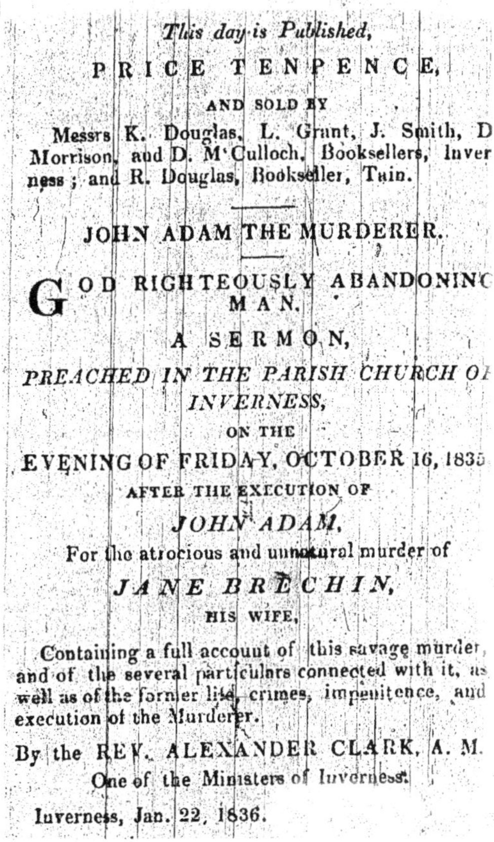

Figure 36: Advertisement for Rev Clark's booklet on the Mulbuie murder, published in January 1836

The issue of the *Inverness Courier* published on Wednesday 20 January 1836 was the first to carry an article on the pamphlet's contents and to provide a lengthy (and somewhat gory) extract on the methodology of the murder. Because of Rev Clark's Aberdeen connection, his sermon and pamphlet was of interest to the *Aberdeen Journal*, which published on Wednesday 27 January 1836 the same article as had appeared in the *Inverness Courier* a week earlier: *The*

Rev Mr Clark of this town, has just published a sermon preached by him on the evening of the 16th October last, after the execution of John Adam in Inverness for the murder of his wife. After some general observations, Mr Clark divides his subject into different heads descriptive of the history and characteristics of the unfortunate man. The first of these is entitled 'John Adam had many advantages for the formation of an amiable and useful character' and presents us with an account of his birth, parentage and early training. The second division continues the narrative and the third exhibits him as 'practiced in the base and treacherous arts of seduction' and the succeeding sections of the discourse accompany the reckless man through the different scenes and gradations of [his] crime to its consummation in the awful guilt of murder and his death on the scaffold. Mr Clark has interspersed various curious biographical particulars throughout his sermon, which had escaped our enquiries, diligent and extensive as they were. It appears that Adam had committed several acts of theft and robbery while in the Army, and had moreover renounced his belief in the Gospel for the principles of deism. Of the murder of poor Jane Brechin there is a very minute account, drawn up chiefly from the confession made by Adam to one of his fellow prisoners in the jail here, previous to his trial. We subjoin an interesting extract:

'Though in that night, there was some small degree of moonlight, still it was so darkened by clouds, as to be generally invisible. After walking together on the highway for a short distance from Kessock Ferry, they struck into the old road, as Adam was anxious to avoid meeting anyone, by taking the most unfrequented route. It soon got quite dark; and as they passed through a wood on this sequestered way, they heard a dismal cry, which resounded fearfully, as it echoed among the trees, and which shook Jane Brechin's heart with terror. It was the hooting of the owl near them, which seemed on that night to have more than its usual melancholy cadence. Jane laid hold of Adam's arm for protection; while she trembled all over. He endeavoured to comfort her by saying that it was only the usual moaning cry of the birds of the night, which were numerous in these plantations. But still it was some time before the melancholy impression died away from her mind. These melancholy cries were but too well adapted to her situation at that moment, when she leaned on the arm of her murderer, who was, under the covert of night, leading her to the place which he had marked out for her grave. After passing the wood, they walked on until the old road again joined the highway. They crossed over, and entered on a path on the other side, leading across the moor to the Church of Urquhart, but which had been for a long time nearly discontinued. They now had got to a lonely part of the extensive common, called Millbuie, a little more than seven miles from Kessock Ferry, being nearly the distance he had more than once told her she had to travel that night, when she became anxious, as the evening advanced. In the distant cottages, no light was to be seen, as the several inhabitants had now barred their doors, and closed their windows, to exclude the chill winds of night, as they prepared to resign themselves to slumber, during the season of darkness. Little did these quiet people dream that, on their peaceful moor, a kind-hearted and unsuspecting woman was then in the power of an unnatural husband, who had enticed her to accompany him thither, that no human ear might hear her dying groan. No earthly witness was near, and the shades of night, together with the solitary nature of the spot, seemed to offer facility for the commission of a deed such as this. Still they had not yet reached the spot marked out by Adam for the murder, which lay a little further onwards; but as his wife stooped to tie her garter, which had loosened by the way, the convenience of the opportunity at once struck him; as, if he assaulted her when standing erect, she might have seen his purpose, and from her bodily strength, made very formidable resistance. In a moment, before she had time to raise herself, he thrust away from under her the leg on which her body leaned, and she fell on her side. "What do you mean, John!" she cried, seizing hold of his vest. "Oh! dear me." She had no time to say more, as he immediately placed his thumbs under her ears, and proceeded to suffocate her. After he thought he had accomplished his purpose, in order to make still more sure, he turned her on her belly, and trampled on her two or three times, until the blood gushed from her ears. Being a strong athletic man, who had fully meditated beforehand the mode of accomplishing this deed, and she taken quite by surprise, he found no difficulty in accomplishing the horrible crime. The scientific manner in which he proceeded showed that he must have well considered and understood the subject previously. As she lay on the cold ground, to all appearance dead, he took from her jacket all the money which she had not already given him, having, doubtless, intended to present to him on their arrival at what she thought was to be their future residence. He took also some small articles, and some letters, which he found with the money. After having now received all which he could ever expect to take from this murdered woman, he proceeded to conceal her remains, as he had formerly intended. He raised the body from the ground, and carried it for some distance, until his progress was interrupted by a dyke, on which he placed it, until he could scramble over. From some feeble remains of life, the body moved, and fell from the dyke, on the opposite side, by the time that he had got within; and, as it fell, a heavy groan escaped from it, which caused him no small alarm. He quickly returned to the side of the fence where the body had fallen, and, as he laid it across the dyke, he perceived by the obscure light which the clouded moon cast over this dismal scene, that the lips still quivered. On observing this, he felt anxious to prevent any further groans escaping from the body, in which he noticed that the vital principle was not yet quite extinguished. By force, he broke the lower jaw at both sides, in his effort to part the chin from the upper jaw, so as to prevent her from uttering any sound which might alarm any person who might happen to be near. Immediately after this last act of cold-blooded violence, she expired, and he carried the body, motionless, to the ruins of an old hut which lay hard by. The hut had been inhabited by some poor person several years before, but, together with a ruined cottage adjoining, had been abandoned; and of both nothing remained but the walls, surrounded on every side by the extensive moorland range of the Millbuie. The nearest inhabited house was a small inn, which stood on the opposite side of the nearest part of the highway, about 270 yards distant from these ruins, and far from any other dwelling; so that the sound of what was going on among these deserted buildings could not reach any house, as, besides the *distance, there was a high fence between the inn and them, by which the common was enclosed. He laid the corpse at full length within this roofless dwelling, and, returning to the outside, he pushed down the wall, so as to cover completely the body deposited there. He thought there were no marks of violence on the remains of his murdered wife, as it was quite unobserved by him at the time, that in his violent effort to hasten the expiration of this injured woman, he had actually broken her lower jaw. And he felt persuaded by the lonely situation of the long-deserted hovel where her earthly frame was buried, that it would never be noticed; and if it should be discovered, he was confident that none would be able to recognise the body, being that of one known to none in the district, while the want of any appearance of external violence would lead the inhabitants to the conclusion that this was the corpse of some stranger who had missed her way, and, during a tempestuous night, had met her death by the wall falling on her as she slept, sheltered by the frail protection from the cold blasts blowing across a particularly exposed and cheerless moorland. – But not only did the state of her face leave clear indication that Jane Brechin had been foully murdered, but, as if the very stones had conspired to produce evidence of the fact, two large stones were so directed in the fall of the wall, as to produce injuries to the head, which tended greatly to confirm suspicion. Thus was consummated the most savage and atrocious murder ever remembered in this country, whether we consider the coolness and length of time in which it premeditated, or the circumstances of treachery and revolting barbarity with which it was perpetrated.*

After having, as he thought, effectively prevented every possibility of his crime being discovered, Adam left this ruined tenement, without the slightest feeling of regret for the fearful sin he had just committed, and without any sorrow whatever for the unhappy end of the woman who so devotedly loved him. But a little after he had reached the highway leading to Dingwall, he thought he saw a man coming to meet him. Having no wish to be met by anyone so near the scene of this horrible deed, he leapt over the dyke and lay for some time within it. When he came on the road, the same figure seemed still to be meeting him; and as he advanced it still kept the same distance. The idea at once entered his mind that this might be an evil spirit; and in a moment, notwithstanding all the boldness with which he used to deride the doctrine of his Bible on these subjects, chilling terror seized on his whole frame. His teeth chattered, every hair on his head stood erect, and the part of his head which was bald, was all bedewed with cold and clammy sweat. He threw from him the smaller articles which he had taken from the murdered body of his wife, whose soul had now gone to bear witness against him, before the highest tribunal; and he tore in pieces the letters on which her name was written, and whose contents he had not time to ascertain, as if he felt a secret dread at being possessed of the property of her whom he had left buried in her blood. The money was in his inside waistcoat pocket, having been put there for safety, and as he felt unwilling to part with it, he ran to Maryburgh as fast as he could. The same terrible apparition seemed still at the same distance, until he reached this place. He then saw no more of it; but as he was trembling all over, he was afraid to go into any house there, lest his appearance might awaken suspicion. At the roadside he sat down, and lighted his pipe, and after remaining for a little time smoking there, he rose and walked to Dingwall. It was considerably later than nine at night when he entered his own house. And, as he had by that time, in some measure, got the better of the fearful impression made on him by what he thought he saw, the young woman who passed there as his wife remarked nothing particular, until he rose after sitting for some time. He then seemed scarcely able to walk across the room from fatigue, which he explained to her by saying that he had walked rather fast on his way home. This was, no doubt, true in some measure, but his exhaustion had been caused, in no small degree, by the death struggle of Jane Brechin, and by his exertion in conveying her murdered body, which was of considerable weight, to the place where he trusted it would be for ever be concealed. The singular apparition which he either saw, or thought he saw, together with the agitation of mind, and fatigue of body which this produced, might have had some share in producing this exhaustion. He carried home with him the identical bundle, and

160

reticule, and umbrella, which his wife had when leaving Inverness. Indeed, the fear which seized him soon after leaving the hut, left him no time to conceal them; and had he thrown them away by the road side, it might have lead to the discovery of the murdered body. On his person, no blood had fallen, save some drops which gushed on his hands, from the nose of the murdered woman, as he carried her motionless body to the place which he had noted as her sepulchre.'

This extract from Rev Clark's pamphlet contains much plausible detail that could only have been known by John Adam and would have been difficult, if not impossible, for anyone else to fabricate from the information that was publicly available at the time. The story, therefore, has to be accepted as a substantially true account of the events leading up to, and immediately following, Jane Brechin's murder – and its *modus operandi.*

What the story also reveals is that the post-mortem medical report compiled by Drs John Jones and William Hall was seriously flawed in two respects that might have gained John an acquittal. The primary cause of Jane's death had been suffocation due to strangulation, not *the violence of the blows the deceased sustained about the head* as reported by the two doctors. Also, Dr Hall had admitted under cross-examination at the trial that Jane's head wounds were probably insufficient to have caused instantaneous death and that *the brain was charged with more dark-coloured blood than was natural, and the lungs were distended, which together were symptomatic of suffocation to a certain degree.* In their defence, it has to be accepted that these doctors would not have been experienced in carrying out post-mortems, especially on the decaying bodies of murder victims. Thus it would perhaps be over-critical to blame them for the confusion over the length of time that Jane's body had lain in the cottage before being discovered – and consequently the true date of the murder. Nevertheless in thinking that the body was only a few days old because air had been excluded, they almost gave John a defendable alibi.

Two days after the *Inverness Courier* had first published Rev Clark's sermon, the *Inverness Journal* of 22 January 1836 carried a review of Rev Clark's pamphlet – stating that it was *a distinct narrative of the life, progress in crime, and death of this unhappy criminal, which he has interwoven with the sermon, so as to present, in regular succession, the striking religious lessons which this melancholy history affords. We think this a very suitable accompaniment to the sermon Mr Clark preached after the execution of Hugh Macleod [the 'Assynt Murderer' executed in 1831]; this being an account of an impenitent criminal, while the other gave a delineation of Macleod's sincere repentance and striking change of mind.* Mimicking the *Inverness Courier* published two days previously, the article then provides *a specimen of the publication* – reproducing an extract from Rev Clark's first-hand account of the execution: *We reached at last the foot of the gibbet; and, after he [John Adam] had ascended the scaffold, a psalm was sung, suitable portions of the inspired word were read, and solemn prayer was offered up for this unhappy criminal. Before he ascended the drop, I asked him whether he had anything further to say to me. In a faint voice he renewed his declaration that he was innocent, which I heard with perfect horror; and, as I really shuddered at the idea of making a man add to his sin, on the very threshold of eternity, I forbore saying any thing further. My interviews had hitherto been strictly alone, and now the last words I ever spoke to him were necessarily in a more public situation. From the feebleness of his voice, when he asserted his innocence, and the pallid appearance of his countenance, I cannot help thinking that if he had been alone, he would then have confessed the whole. For he began now to fear, at last, that he was to die, and, as he ascended the drop, he evidently trembled much. Up to this moment, every trivial circumstance seemed to strengthen his expectations that he would not suffer death that day; as, for instance, that the usual cap worn by condemned criminals was not put upon his head when about to leave his cell. – When he stood upon the drop, he turned quite round, with his face to the assembled magnitude, as if he was anxious to turn away his eyes from the quarter to which he looked, when he ascended the narrow stair leading from the scaffold. What object was that from which his eyes turned, at this solemn moment, when the executioner proceeded to put on his head the cap, which, pulled down over his face, was intended to conceal the effects produced on his countenance by the last struggles of death? It was the road along which he walked with his murdered wife, on that dismal night, and the lonely Millbuie in which he had buried her motionless body. The same shrinking feelings which seized him, when the lonely hut was pointed out from the road, as he was carried from Dingwall to Inverness, seemed to have caused him to then fall round after having ascended the drop, in order to escape the recollections of that fearful night, which this view seemed eminently adapted to awaken; and after the executioner had drawn the cap over his eyes, and adjusted the rope, he gave the signal, by dropping the handkerchief – the platform fell – his dying struggle was severe – and, in a short time, his spirit passed to meet, as Judge of all the earth, the redeemer whom he once professed, but afterwards frequently and wickedly blasphemed. Death came to him unexpectedly; as, though often warned, he had the same illusion floating before his mind, that he would not be actually executed, however near he was brought to the verge of life. It was an extremely melancholy spectacle, and one of which I earnestly pray I may never see the like again. As he had lived making lies his great resource, so he died trusting to the same defence. The very last words he uttered in this world were evidently untrue. And in his case, death appeared as the entrance to a gloomy and forlorn eternity, over which no single gleam of hope was seen to shine. No expression of sympathy, in his fate, could be discerned in the immense multitude which surrounded the execution. All seemed pervaded with one sentiment of horror at the crime of which he had been guilty, and awe at this fearful example of impenitence in death.*

This extract seems to confirm that John Adam believed that he had been convicted on purely circumstantial evidence and would ultimately be reprieved if he remained impenitent. Although the road out of North Kessock and some of the lower slopes of the Mulbuie are visible from the Longman, the site of the murder is not. Despite Rev Clark's contention that John looked away from the view over the Beauly Firth because of the memories it evoked, what seems more feasible is that he was looking around, probably by then quite desperately, for any signs of the arrival of a royal warrant for his pardon.

(ii) Phrenological Examinations

Although it is stated in the various accounts of the execution and its aftermath that John Adam's body was put in a coffin to be transported back to the Inverness Tolbooth and buried, he was not immediately interred. It was customary at the time for the bodies of geniuses and convicted criminals, such as murderers, to be subjected to phrenological measurement. Phrenology was the 'science' that studied the relationship between the measurable characteristics of a body, particularly the head, and that person's character, attributes and behaviour. In particular, though always contentious, it was believed that the heads of all murderers possessed characteristic features that could explain why they committed such crimes. In consequence, there was much demand for access to the body after a hanging.

In the case of John Adam, it had been agreed that Sir George Mackenzie of the University of Edinburgh, assisted by Dr John Inglis Nicol of Inverness and Procurator-Fiscal Hugh Cameron of Dingwall, could take a plaster cast (death mask) of his head. This was performed in the Inverness Tolbooth and the initial results were first published in an *Inverness Courier* article of Wednesday 21 October, which reported: *The phrenological developments of Adam corresponded very closely with his character and dispositions. The organ of firmness was so prominent as to give the head something of a conical appearance: conscientiousness was in the same degree deficient, while secretiveness and amativeness [desire to indulge in sexual passion] were very large.*

The death mask (and, according to some reports, John's head) was then taken to Edinburgh but was damaged on one side during transit. However, it (and/or the head) was measured as accurately as possible and the data compared with that of other murderers. A full thirteen-page report was published in March 1836 in the *Phrenological Journal and Miscellany*[66]. According to this report, phrenology could distinguish between three classes of murderer: those who commit the crime as a release of a lust for blood; those who commit the crime in response to a provocation; and those who commit the crime as the readiest way of removing an obstacle to the achievement of an end. Murderers in the first class were recognised as possessing very prominent organs of destructiveness and combativeness. Murderers in the second class showed no extreme development of any organ but their destructiveness was readily aroused by resentment or jealousy.

The third class of murderer was distinguished by highly developed organs of firmness and amativeness. John Adam's character and cerebral development showed him to belong mainly to this third class. On a scale of 0-20, John's highest organ development scores were: amativeness, firmness and self-esteem – 19; cautiousness, love of approbation and secretiveness – 18; acquisitiveness, concentrativeness, destructiveness, philoprogenitiveness and veneration – 17. In the words of the report: *Our readers will easily perceive how closely the particulars given above correspond with the leading features in the development of Adam's head. The effects of amativeness, firmness and self-esteem, which are the largest organs, appear in every step of his history. Secretiveness large and well-cultivated, combined with conscientiousness only rather full [it scored 13] and self-esteem large, was the origin of his unprincipled fabrication of lies, and disregard of the rights of others when placed in competition with his own. Veneration was sufficient to antagonise self-esteem so far as to render his behaviour respectful; although being associated with moderate wonder [which scored 12] and reflection [no score given], it was never strongly directed to any religious object. Under the dictates of self-esteem and secretiveness, combined with a moderate endowment of the reflective faculties, he appears to have thought his schemes and movements unfathomable by other men; and in this way cautiousness was apt to be on some occasions lulled into repose. The obstinacy with which he denied his guilt was very remarkable; and in accordance with this, and the general tenor of his character through life, the organ of firmness (as is remarked in the Inverness Courier) was so prominent as to give his head something of a conical appearance.*

Despite its content of what would now be regarded as phrenological nonsense, this report is of considerable value in other respects. In particular, it contains a full transcription of the only authentic account of John's early life in Lintrathen, written specifically for this report by the parish minister, Rev Francis Cannan[5].

This report is also the only source document that provides a plausible reason why John Adam murdered Jane Brechin. It reveals, from an unstated source, that John: *had spoken to Dorothy Elliott of a plan he had of going to America to settle as an emigrant; and had proposed she should return to her family until he was settled, when he would come back and marry her.* Furthermore, it postulates that: *the murder appears to have been deliberately and skilfully planned; and every thing seems to have been arranged for his departure before it was committed ... the idea of murdering his victim arose much less from any direct malevolence or cruelty towards her personally, than from his being unable to devise any better way by which he could rid himself of an obstacle to the gratification of his selfish desires ... the two motives by which Adam was chiefly actuated, appear to have been, 1st, a desire to get possession of the woman's money; and 2nd, a wish to free himself of her society, which was far inferior in attraction to that of Dorothy Elliott.* Thus, only the unpredictably early discovery of Jane's body, which had led to his early arrest, had thwarted (in phrenological parlance) 'the achievement of his end'.

If this interpretation of events is accepted as John's motive for the murder, it raises the question as to whether Dorothy Elliott was aware of the entire plan, or just part of it. If the former, she would have been 'art and part' to the murder. However, there is no hint in the case documentation that the law authorities held any such suspicions during her precognition, nor was she called to give testimony at the trial. Dorothy had stated in her precognition that she had decided to go home to Derbyshire unless John married her and that John had agreed that she could go in May and would follow her and marry her in England. This suggests that John, not expecting the body to be discovered before May, was planning to immigrate to America with some immediacy after the murder, but not necessarily that Dorothy was aware of this. Thus, despite the temptation to think that the marriage and murder could have been jointly planned for the monetary gain, the evidence for Dorothy having any part is not strong.

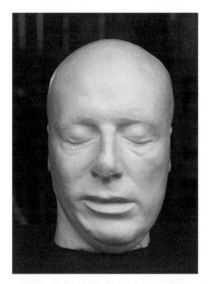

Figure 37: John Adam's death mask– currently on loan
to the Scottish National Portrait Gallery (John Adam
1804-1835, Collection of the University of Edinburgh)

An engraving of John Adam's death mask[67] was published in
1841 in *The Phrenological Journal and Magazine of Moral Science*
although the article makes little reference to the case. The death
mask still survives. It was stored until 1886 in the museum of the
Edinburgh Phrenological Society in Chambers Street, a building
which is still adorned on its facade by a number of sculptured heads.
It was then transferred to the Anatomy Department of the Faculty of
Medicine of the University of Edinburgh and was displayed in 1988
in an exhibition of death and life masks of the famous and infamous[68]
held under the auspices of a programme entitled 'Scotland's Cultural
Heritage' in the Tron Kirk in Edinburgh. The mask has subsequently
been transferred on long-term loan into the safe keeping of the
Scottish National Portrait Gallery in Edinburgh, where it is currently
on display[69]. Unfortunately, the mask whose photograph is featured in
the programme of the 1988 'Scotland's Cultural Heritage' exhibition
bears no resemblance to the mask on display in the Gallery.

(iii) Multiple Burials

There is no 'official' record of John Adam's death, nor is his burial recorded in the Inverness old parish registers. However, it can be assumed that his body was interred during the evening of Friday 16 October, after his death mask had been taken and the possible removal of his head had been completed. In Scotland, the remains of an executed person could not be buried in consecrated ground and it was customary for unrepentant murderers to be buried upright in chloride of lime so that their soul could never be 'at rest'. It is most likely that John Adam was buried in this way – one account, written in 1888, refers to him being *interred standing in a deep grave*[70]. This account also declares that the flagstones of the passageway between the Tolbooth and the Courthouse were replaced over the grave . . . *and that was the last of the miserable man.*

But it wasn't! What the writer of that article [probably John Noble] did not know was that John Adam had remained upright in his grave for only twelve years. During 1848-53 the site of the Inverness Burgh Tolbooth, near the Steeple in Bridge Street, was redeveloped and John's bones had been dug up. By this time a County prison had been built in the North Tower of Inverness Castle. John, however, was not re-buried there. Instead, he was placed under the charge of the new Inverness Burgh Police force which had been created in October 1847 and whose new headquarters were opened in 1848 in Castle Wynd. John's remains were re-buried under one of the cells and, although there seems to be no reference in either the Inverness Burgh Council[71] or Prison Board[72] minutes of the actual date, an article published on 12 February 1999 in *The Scotsman* states that *in 1853 the body – minus the head which had been sent to Edinburgh for phrenology tests – was re-interred in Castle Wynd.*

The Inverness Burgh police headquarters in Castle Wynd were demolished in 1911 and a new building was erected on the same site. During the demolition, human bones were discovered and the work was temporarily stopped until investigations revealed that these were the remains of John Adam. It was ordained that the bones should be re-buried under the new building. The source of this information[73] is an annotation written in 1943 on a copy of John Noble's pamphlet[70] by the then Deputy Chief Constable of Inverness Burgh Police, William Dalgleish. He wrote: *When the present police office in Castle Wynd was dismantled in 1911-12 for re-building, human bones were found under the floor of one of the cells. The fact was reported to the Crown Authorities and a search of the Town Council minutes revealed that when the then police force moved from the Tolbooth at the Steeple to the original police office in Castle Wynd about 1846, the remains of [John] Adam were also removed. The Crown Authorities ordered that these human bones be re-interred under the new building and this was done early in 1912 and they now lie under the concrete floor of the room in the basement known as the 'Furnace Room'.*

William Dalgleish was probably not entirely accurate with his dates but, once again, there appears to be no surviving 'official' evidence to verify or refute his annotation. Indeed there are widely conflicting accounts, for example, in articles published on 12 February 1999, *The Scotsman* states: *In 1921 workmen unearthed the bones;* whilst *The Herald* states: *In 1914 workmen at Castle Wynd found a skeleton thought to be Adam's and it was reburied in another site within Castle Wynd.*

John Adam's remains were again disturbed in 1963 when the centre of Inverness was redeveloped to accommodate the approaches to the new Ness Bridge. By this time, the prison system had been re-organised and HM Prison had been built at Porterfield. Consideration may have been given to re-interring John's remains in Porterfield but, once again, the bones seem to have been considered the responsibility of the Burgh and were kept (allegedly on a shelf in a cupboard) in the Burgh police's temporary headquarters in the former Dr Bell's school at Farraline Park [now the Central Library]. The Burgh and County police forces were merged into the Inverness Constabulary in 1968. In conjunction with Scottish local government re-organisation in 1975, Northern Constabulary was created by merger of all the Highland police forces and new headquarters were built on the Old Perth Road, Inverness. John's remains were re-interred in a plywood box under the foundations of the cell block. According to Inspector Colin Sutherland, quoted in *The Scotsman* article of 12 February 1999, *an unmarked grave was dug and the bones laid at a depth from which they would never be recovered.* How prophetic were those words!

The headquarters of Northern Constabulary were demolished and replaced in the late 1990s. The site of the cell block was scheduled to be redeveloped as a car park but, as had been stated by Inspector Sutherland, the exact location of John's remains had not been marked in 1975 and nobody could be found who could recall seeing them being re-interred. Predictably, the story soon gained the attention of the national press. *The Herald* broke the news on 2 May 1997 with a lengthy article that described how the Northern Constabulary was s*et to launch a search for human remains under its own doorstep* and quoted Inspector Willie MacLean explaining pessimistically that *we will be taking steps to locate them [the bones] – if they exist at all now.* The story was also carried under the headline 'Murderer on the move for 163 years' by *The Scotsman* of 15 April 1998. Featuring photographs of the death mask (the one on display in the Scottish National Portrait Gallery) and of the old police station in Castle Wynd, the article proclaimed that John Adam had become *more famous in death than in life ... (having) ... passed into folklore as the man who has not been allowed to rest in peace ... (having) ... been buried four times in different locations – and his remains could be moved again this year.* There were also some comments from Sheila MacKay of the Inverness Local History Forum, who suggested that the killer *be given a Christian burial, with the grave marked as a tourist attraction.*

In early 1999, Northern Constabulary engaged Oceanfix International, a company expert in hi-tech ground-radar surveying, to probe the site – but the bones remained elusive. *The Scotsman* had a field day on 12 February 1999 when it wrote: *More than 160 years after being convicted for murder, John Adam is still evading police. It had been assumed that the notorious wife killer had spent the last quarter of a century securely accommodated in the cell block of Northern Constabulary headquarters, until they went to find him. Despite an extensive investigation, he remains a missing person.* On the same day, *The Herald,* under the headline: 'Police hot on the trail of 19th century killer', wrote with similar rhetoric: *Police in Inverness were in their cells yesterday searching for a wife-murderer they thought had been held securely since he was taken to police headquarters twenty-four years ago.* Both papers also carried photographs of Inspector Willie MacLean and Peter Simpkins of Oceanfix searching the rubble of the old cells for the elusive bones.

The *Inverness Courier* was less sarcastic on 12 February 1999 with a front page headline: 'Car park will cover hanged man's bones' and an explanation that Northern Constabulary had brought in specialists with ground-probing radar equipment but had decided that: *the bones of John Adam ... should not be moved from their present site below a cell in the force's Perth Road headquarters in Inverness. Instead, the cells are to be demolished and replaced by a car park ... a plaque will be laid in the tarmac to mark his final resting place and a low-key religious ceremony may be held.* The *Inverness Courier* article also carried another reaction from Sheila MacKay of the Inverness Local History Forum, who said: *The police have done a tremendous amount of work researching what happened to John Adam. It is a very reasonable decision that he should be kept here with a plaque to mark the spot.* Then, seeking again to promote local tourism, she called for *the cast of Adam's head which was made for Edinburgh University for research into phrenology – the study of bumps on the head – and the death mask to be returned to Inverness.*

Two weeks later on 26 February 1999, *The Scotsman* similarly wrapped up its coverage of the search for John Adam's remains, informing that: *An extensive inquiry has failed to track down a wife murderer who is still evading police 160 years after being hanged* adding that *the grave is thought to be deep enough not to be disturbed when demolition work starts. It is intended to mark the likely grave area with a plaque and rose.*

Thus, despite the extensive efforts of the police, John Adam's remains are undiscovered. Having been moved five times since 1835, he is presumed to lie deep under the car park of the new headquarters of the Northern Constabulary on the Old Perth Road, Inverness. Although there is no report of a religious ceremony being held, a small memorial plaque stands in the car park in the approximate vicinity of the cell block of the 1975-1999 building.

Figure 38: The memorial plaque to John Adam located in the police headquarters car park at Perth Road, Inverness

(iv) The Red Barn Murder

Whilst John Adam's motive and method had both been clarified after the event, the question of how he conceived the initial idea had not. One possible answer may lie in the similarities between the 'Mulbuie murder' and the 'Red Barn murder' of Maria Marten in Suffolk in 1827. Like the Mulbuie murder, this murder was also the outcome of a love triangle and became widely reported – not just because of the morbidity of the murder itself, but for the many intriguing peripheral elements and revelations that began to appear after the execution.

Maria Marten was born in Polstead on 24 July 1801, the daughter of Thomas Marten, a mole-catcher, and his wife, Grace. When Maria was only nine years old, Grace died and Thomas Marten soon re-married a young girl named Ann (who was said to be little older than Maria). Maria grew up to be an intelligent and good-looking young woman, who attracted the attentions of wealthy young men. At age seventeen, she became involved with Thomas Corder, the son of a wealthy farmer, and gave birth to an illegitimate son who died in infancy. Although now a 'fallen woman', Maria then had a secret liaison with a wealthy gentleman named Peter Matthews by whom she had a second son, Thomas Henry. There was no marriage but Peter provided Maria with a regular allowance for the upkeep of his child.

In 1824, the 23 year-old Maria took up with William Corder, Thomas' youngest brother who was now the wealthy sole owner of the farm as his father and brothers had all died. He promised to marry Maria but his mother disapproved and he always found an excuse to delay the wedding. Maria had a third child in 1827 but it died shortly after birth. Amongst the many mysteries of the case is whether the child had been killed by William and Maria and where the body was buried – the couple had pretended to take it to Sudbury for burial, but it was probably buried in a field.

William Corder was not well liked. He had not got on well with his father or brothers, but was quite attached to his mother. He was nicknamed 'Foxey' because he was given to stealing, lying and womanising. On one occasion, after stealing some pigs, one witness is reputed to have declared: *I'll be damned if he [Corder] will not be hung some of these days.*

On 18 May 1827, Maria Marten left home to meet her lover, William Corder, in a large wooden barn which they regularly used to conduct their liaison. It stood on Barnfield Hill, about half a mile from the Martens' cottage, and had a red tiled roof which gave it the name of the 'Red Barn'. She believed that William Corder was meeting her in order to elope to Ipswich, because the local constable was rumoured to have obtained a warrant to prosecute her for bearing illegitimate children. She was never seen or heard from again, although several letters were sent by William Corder to her parents, in which he stated that he and Maria were now married and would soon return to resume occupation of his farm. In these letters he fabricated many excuses for Maria's silence.

In December 1827 Maria's step-mother, Ann Marten, started to have dreams that Maria had been murdered and was buried in the Red Barn. In April 1828 she finally persuaded Thomas Marten to search the barn. Prodding the floor of the barn with a mole-spud, he found a soft spot and dug down to discover a body stuffed into a sack. A green silk handkerchief showed through and Thomas recognised it as one belonging to William Corder and which Maria was wearing when she left the house. He left the body where it lay and called the coroner from Bury St Edmunds, who quickly summoned a jury to an inquest at the Cock Inn in Polstead. Maria's sister identified the body from a missing tooth and her clothing and belongings. Other evidence was given which implicated William Corder, who was traced through a number of addresses until he was found in Brentford, where he and his wife, Mary Moore, were running a boarding house for females at the Grove House, Ealing Lane. He was arrested on 23 April 1828 and transmitted to the county jail in Bury St Edmunds. Mary, whom William had met through a matrimonial advertisement posted in a pastry cook's shop in Fleet Street, and whom he had married in Holborn in November 1827, was initially under the impression that the charge against him was bigamy.

The trial at Bury St Edmunds was initially scheduled for Monday 4 August 1828 but it was delayed until Thursday 7 August because of the huge crowds that had gathered in the town. In the event, entry to the court was by ticket only and women were not admitted. William Corder pleaded not guilty. Although there was no doubt that Maria had been murdered, there was difficulty in determining the actual cause of death due to the decomposition of the body. Cuts in Maria's clothing suggested a stabbing but they could have been made when Thomas Marten found the body with his mole-spud. Wounds to the head indicated that Maria might have been shot. William Corder's green handkerchief had been tied tightly round Maria's neck, so strangulation could not be ruled out. The handkerchief had been used to drag the body across the barn floor, so Maria could have been buried alive and died of suffocation.

The trial lasted two days and, despite failure to establish the cause of death, William Corder was found guilty on evidence that was entirely circumstantial. The judge, Chief Baron Alexander, passed sentence in words remarkably similar to those that would be pronounced by Lord Moncrieff to John Adam seven years later: *My advice to you is, not to flatter yourself with the slightest hope of mercy on earth. You sent this unfortunate young woman to her account, with all her imperfections upon her head, without allowing her any time for preparation. She had not time to lift up her eyes to a throne of grace, to implore mercy and forgiveness for her manifold transgressions – she had no time allowed her to repent of her sins – no time granted to throw herself upon her knees, to implore pardon at the Eternal Throne! The same measure which you meted to her is not meted out to you again. A small interval is allowed you for preparation. Let me earnestly entreat you to use it well – the scene of this world closes upon you – but, I hope, another and a better world will open to your view. Remember the lessons of religion, which you, doubtless, received in your childhood – consider the effects which may be produced by a hearty and sincere repentance – listen to the voice of the ministers of religion who will, I trust, advise and console you, so that you may be able to meet with becoming resignation and fortitude that dreadful ordeal which you will have shortly to undergo.*

Nothing remains now for me to do but to pass upon you the awful sentence of the law, and that sentence is: That you be taken back to the prison from whence you came, and that you be taken from thence, on Monday next, to a place of execution, and that you there be hanged by the neck until you are dead ; and that your body shall afterwards be dissected and anatomized ; and may the Lord God Almighty, of his infinite goodness, have mercy on your soul!

During the evening before the execution, William Corder issued a detailed confession in which he wrote that he and Maria had quarrelled, in particular about the burial of their child and whether

Figure 39: The execution of William Corder in Bury St Edmund's on 11 August 1828 (unknown artist)

the grave might be discovered. [The fate of the child was perhaps preying on Maria's conscience and she may have declared a wish to confess to the authorities.] A scuffle had broken out and he had taken his pistol from his jacket pocket and fired. Maria had instantly fallen dead. William had then dug a hole in the barn floor and had buried Maria there.

William Corder was hanged in Bury St. Edmunds shortly after noon on 11 August 1828. Estimates of the numbers present to view the spectacle ranged from 7,000 to 20,000. The execution itself seems to have been less than well conducted. Whilst William Corder was suspended from the noose, the executioner, John Foxton, had to grasp him around the waist to finish the task. After hanging for an hour, the body was cut down and put on public display until 6pm.

Several death masks were then prepared by John Childs of Bungay, a well-known Suffolk printer. One was sent to the noted phrenologist, Dr Johann Spurzheim, who reported: *among the animal feelings, acquisitiveness, secretiveness and combativeness predominated; amativeness and philoprogenitiveness, destructiveness and cautiousness came next; love of approbation and adhesiveness followed; and finally, inhabitiveness and self-esteem were very small. In the sincipital region, marvellousness and imitation were the largest;*

then came hope; afterwards followed benevolence, veneration and ideality: firmness and conscientiousness were very small. William Corder's death mask is still on display at Moyse's Hall museum, Bury St Edmunds.

Next day William Corder's body was dissected by George Creed, a surgeon in the Bury & Suffolk General Hospital, in front of an audience of physicians and students from Cambridge University. The body and every organ were found to be perfectly healthy. Some of the physicians then carried out a phrenological examination of the skull and declared it to be: *profoundly developed in the areas of secretiveness, acquisitiveness, destructiveness, philoprogenitiveness and imitativeness [amativeness] with little evidence of benevolence or veneration.* More bizarrely, George Creed kept and preserved the scalp (with the right ear attached), the skeleton and a piece of the skin – which was subsequently tanned and used to bind a book about the murder written in 1828 by James Curtis[74]. The book is held in the Moyse's Hall museum and is inscribed: *The binding of this book is the skin of the murderer William Corder taken from his body and tanned by myself in the year 1828. George Creed, Surgeon to the Suffolk Hospital.*

Apart from the phrenological investigations, the Mulbuie murder and the Red Barn murder have many other similarities. These include a marriage promise, illegitimate children, prophetic dreams, prediction of death by execution, identification of the body by a missing tooth, uncertainty over the cause of death and committal by purely circumstantial evidence.

However, there is a further twist in the story that reveals a remarkable similarity to the Mulbuie murder. It appears that Maria's step-mother, Ann Marten, was also having an affair with William Corder. Maria seems to have found out and a plan was drawn up to lure her to her death (just as Jane Brechin was lured by John Adam). However, Maria was probably lured to her death with the full knowledge of the 'other woman' – whereas Dorothy Elliott does not seem to have been aware of John Adam's plan to murder Jane Brechin.

After the murder, William Corder married Mary Moore – a marriage that was discovered by the scorned Ann Marten in December 1827. In revenge, she is thought to have concocted her dreams – well aware that Maria's body was buried in the Red Barn and unearthing it would inevitably lead to the conviction and execution of William Corder.

After William Corder's execution there was a great deal of media hype and a flourishing market for memorabilia, for example: a man named James Catnach sold over a million broadsheets; James Curtis wrote his best-selling book; pieces of the hangman's rope sold for a guinea each; a lock of Maria's hair sold for two guineas; the Red Barn was stripped by souvenir hunters; Maria's gravestone was completely chipped away for gruesome mementos; and numerous plays and songs were composed. It is probably overstretching the remarkable similarities between the two murders to postulate that John Adam conceived the murder of Jane Brechin from knowledge of the Red Barn murder. However, he must have been aware of it.

(v) Other Accounts of the Mulbuie Murder

The uxoricide [murder of a wife] of Jane Brechin has featured in several subsequent accounts – although none have provided any serious analysis or re-assessment of the evidence. A selection is given below.

Excluding the publication in January 1836 of extracts from Rev Alexander Clark's sermon by the *Inverness Courier* and the *Aberdeen Journal*, the first commentary on the murder was contained in the thirteen-page article published in 1836 in *The Phrenological Journal and Miscellany*[66]. The introductory pages of this article contain summaries of the murder and the trial, but concentrate mainly on the upbringing and character of John Adam – including Rev Francis Cannan's excellent account of John's early life in Lintrathen[5]. This article was also the first to reveal John's intention of immigrating to America – an important element in understanding his motive for committing the murder. An abridgement of this article was synchronously published by the *Legal Observer (or Journal of*

The Mulbuie Murder.

LIFE AND TRIAL OF

JOHN ADAM,

AT INVERNESS CIRCUIT COURT,

On September 1835,

FOR THE MURDER OF HIS WIFE,

JANE BRECHIN,

CONTAINING A REPORT OF THE EVIDENCE,
AN ACCOUNT OF THE EXECUTION,
THE SUBSEQUENT FULL DISCLOSURE OF THE CRIME,
AND EXTRACTS FROM THE
SERMON BY REV. MR CLARK ON THE EVENING
OF THE EXECUTION.

INVERNESS:

JOHN NOBLE, CASTLE STREET.

Figure 40: The title page of John Noble's booklet on the life and death of John Adam, published in 1888 (reproduced by permission of the National Library of Scotland)

Jurisprudence)[75] under the heading of 'Remarkable Trials; Case of John Adam for Murder'.

In 1888, a fifty-one-page pamphlet entitled *The Mulbuie Murder* and subtitled *Life and Trial of John Adam at Inverness Circuit Court, on September 1835, for the murder of his wife, Jane Brechin* was published by John Noble of Castle Street, Inverness[70]. It is not clear whether John Noble also wrote the pamphlet, but he probably did because he was a prolific writer (and publisher), particularly well-known for his *Miscellanea Invernessiana: with a bibliography of Inverness newspapers and periodicals.*

If at times over-embellished with imaginative scene-setting passages, this is a highly readable account of the murder of Jane Brechin. It is also extensive in its coverage, with chapters on: Discovery of a Murder; Early Life and Adventures of John Adam; John Adam's Duplicity; Adam under Suspicion; The Trial; Verdict and Sentence; The Condemned Cell; The Execution; The Funeral Sermon; and The Crime Disclosed. However, it contains some minor errors – for example: it refers to William Smart of Cairnbank as *Mr Stewart of Carrisbank*; it states that the trial *had lasted more than two hours* – confusing 12.30 pm with 12.30 am on the next day; and it was unaware that John's remains had been moved from their original burial site. Despite these errors of detail, it is well researched from the newspaper reports of the day and the precognition and trial papers. Clearly, John Noble also had access to a copy of Rev Clark's sermon, providing numerous and apparently verbatim passages from that publication, which he refers to as a 'pamphlet'. Indeed, he provides a facsimile of the title page of the pamphlet and reproduces its preface: *It reflects no small honour on the criminal jurisprudence of our country, that in the case of an unknown woman, barbarously murdered, the body was identified, and the murderer committed for trial, little more than 60 days after the corpse has been found; and that, when more than common ingenuity had been employed, to render such discovery for ever impossible. But while we give to human instrumentality its due need of praise, in pursuing this judicial investigation, there seems throughout the whole, an extraordinary interposition of Divine*

Providence as has often been remarked in other cases, for bringing to light the shedder of blood. I have met with very few narratives more adapted to be extremely useful, especially in warning those who are just resigning themselves to the rapid currency of sensual indulgence.

This pamphlet is also very significant in one other respect. When discussing John Adam's duplicity and his first trip south to borrow money from Jane Brechin in the autumn of 1834, it records: *To add to his anxiety his pretended wife was approaching her confinement, and in short he began to find his position becoming intolerable.* Where John Noble came upon the information that Dorothy Elliott was pregnant is not known – it certainly is not mentioned in any of the contemporaneous newspaper reports. Furthermore, it is astonishing that none of the precognosed witnesses, especially the Urquharts in whose house Dorothy was living, made any statement to that effect.

It might be thought that the centenary of the murder would have provided an opportunity for the newspapers to commemorate the event. However, this does not seem to have been the case. The *Inverness Journal* carried an article in its '100 years ago' column entitled 'The Millbuie Murderer in Irons' on 2 July 1935 – but, without any contextual introduction or attribution, it simply replicates the short article about John's confinement in Inverness Tolbooth that was published in the *Inverness Courier* on 1 July 1835. Similarly, the *Inverness Courier* in its '100 years ago' column carried a much abridged version of the article on 'The Execution of John Adam, Inverness' that it had published on 21 October 1835. The only addition was a tailpiece which stated that: *The account of Adam's execution states that he confessed his guilt to a fellow-prisoner.* Why that statement was included is not clear – the original article does not refer to John's confession to John Sutherland, his fellow-prisoner.

A number of true murder-genre books have featured the murder of Jane Brechin. Many of these feature articles written by William Roughead, the well-known Scottish lawyer and amateur criminologist. For example, *Malice Domestic* written by him and published in 1928 contains a chapter entitled *The Malbuie [sic] murder; or, when Adam delved.* The same chapter appears in his book entitled *Reprobates*

Reviewed published in 1941; and it also appears as a chapter entitled the 'The Mulbuie Murder' in the *Fireside Mystery Book* edited by Frank Owen and published in 1947 in New York.

William Roughead's much reproduced account relies heavily on John Noble's 1888 pamphlet[70] which he describes as John Adam's *official biography*, in consequence perpetuating its many errors – as well as introducing several more. For example: he conjectures that Jane Stewart and John Campbell had discovered Jane's corpse *at the close of the day* – it was in the early morning; he refers to Dorothy Elliott as *the one fair daughter of a well-to-do innkeeper* – she had a sister and her father was a lead miner; and he claims that John's 'sketch' *did not appear in print till after his demise* – it was published two days before the execution. He is also not averse to the introduction of additional 'facts' to enliven the story, for example, in stating that with his dying breath John *protested his innocence, declaring that on the ground he would meet with God*. His description of Dorothy Elliott's possible pregnancy in the autumn of 1834 is also novel: *Mrs Anderson's state of health betokened an increase of responsibility and expense in the near future*. Nevertheless, like its source, it remains an entertaining and highly readable account.

More recently, Norman Newton in his *The Life and Times of Inverness* published in 1996, devotes seven pages to the trial and hanging of John Adam – leaning heavily on the various accounts published in the *Inverness Courier*. He also refers to the several re-interments of John's remains, notes the phrenological measurements of the death mask, and comments entertainingly on the life and extraordinary emoluments of Donald Ross, the Inverness Burgh executioner until 1833. In the absence of information on the executioner of John Adam, Norman Newton suggests that Donald Ross may have been re-called or a hangman imported. The latter was the case, his name being John Murdoch.

A short unpublished account entitled *The Story of John Adam: The Mulbuie Murderer* was written in 1999 by Colin Sutherland[76]. It is based on research of the original 19th century papers and also refs to John Sutherland's account of the murder methodology. It is notable in being one of the few accounts to raise the issue of the use of the out-dated ordeal of the bier-right as a legal instrument.

Molly Whittington-Egan in her *Classic Scottish Murder Stories* published in 2007, includes a fourteen-page chapter entitled 'The Battered Bride'. Whilst it draws its content mainly from the already published accounts, this is an excellent, if somewhat simplistic, well-written essay. It is another of the few accounts to describe the 'trial by touch' (bier-right) and is one of three accounts to note the possibility of Dorothy Elliott being pregnant in the autumn of 1834. It also refers to Dorothy's pregnancy when John was arrested in April 1835: *Poor, pregnant Dorothy, his wife in all but formality, who had hoped for marriage, was astonished by the revelations and was left behind with the Urquharts to comfort her while Adam was hurried in handcuffs to the Town House.*

Finally, it is noteworthy that John Noble's 1888 pamphlet has recently been reproduced in *The Making of the Modern Law: Trials 1600-1926* published by Lightning Source UK Ltd in 2012.

(vi) Where are they now?

John Adam was the father of at least three illegitimate children. The first, Helen Adam (baptised Hellen Adam), was born in Lintrathen on 25 June 1826. Her mother, Margaret Ogilvy, was deaf and dumb. As had been promised by Margaret's father at her baptism, Helen appears to have been brought up in Lintrathen. At the time of the 1841 census[77] they were both resident in the parish, Margaret at Kinloch where she was a housekeeper for her father, and Helen, aged fourteen, with her uncle at Bottom farm. Margaret died on 4 November 1847. The record in the Lintrathen old parish register of burials[2] seems to give an erroneous age and provides a somewhat odd explanation of the cause of death: *Margaret Ogilvy, Iornstench inflammation of bowels (aged 54). Dumb.* ['Iornstench' is probably a miss-spelling of 'ironstench' – more commonly referred to as 'ironsmell'].

In her youth, Helen Adam obtained employment on the Airlie estate as a dairymaid and at Denhead, Kirriemuir, as a linen weaver. However, in *circa* 1865 she became a general farm servant at West Mains of Gardyne in the parish of Kirkden, near Forfar, before moving in *circa* 1885 to keep house for a widowed eighty year-old named Carnegie Herald at West Hills farm in the parish of Carmyllie. She was never married and died of a cerebral embolism in the Almshouse in Kirriemuir, aged 76, on 20 August 1902. The death certificate[78] names the informant as Annie Cook, Matron of the Almshouse, and records Helen's father only as *Adam (deceased)*.

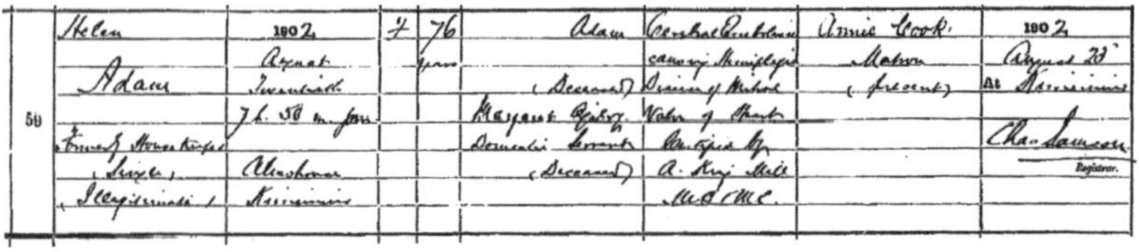

Figure 41: Helen Adam's death record in the Kirriemuir old parish register of August 1902 (reproduced with permission of the Church of Scotland)

John Adam's second child, John, was born on 18 July 1826. Although he was brought up in Dundee by his mother, Betty (or Biddy) Easson, he seems to have returned to Lintrathen at the age of about twelve to work as an agricultural labourer with his uncle, Alexander Adam, at Cantsmill farm in the parish of Kingoldrum [adjacent to Lintrathen]. At the same time, Biddy seems to have moved to Kirriemuir where she worked as a domestic servant at Southmuir farm. In 1858 John was working as a ploughman at Broughty farm in the parish of Alyth, Perthshire, when he married the 23 year-old Ann Cargill on 30 July at Easter Craig in the parish of Glenisla. The marriage certificate[78] describes John's father as: *John Adam, Soldier (deceased)*. At first they lived in a cottar's cottage at Broughty and later in the old farm house, known as Nether Balloch. John's mother, Biddy Easson, lived with them until she died in the 1870s. John and Ann had four children, all born at Broughty: Betsy (born in 1860); James (1864); William (1867); and Mary-Ann (1871). John died of senile decay, aged 74, at Nether Balloch on 11 April 1900 [the death certificate[78] leaves his father's name blank] and his wife, Ann, died of stomach cancer on 8 October 1910 in Cairnleith, Alyth. Several of Betsy and James's children had lived with John and Ann during the 1890s. With certainty, John Adam's genes still survive from this branch of his 'family'.

John Adam's third child, also John, was baptised on 30 November 1830 in Chapel of Garioch, Aberdeenshire. Nothing is known of his mother, Janet Laing, other than she was an unmarried woman living in Bogranie and that there was a witness at the baptism named Alexander Laing. They do not seem to have remained in Chapel of Garioch and it is not known what happened to them.

James Adam, John's younger brother, remained as the tenant at Craigieloch farm in Lintrathen. Although he had visited John in Inverness Tolbooth after the trial, it is not recorded whether he witnessed the execution. His mother, Betty, remained in Craigieloch until she died there on 15 November 1845. The Lintrathen old parish register of deaths[2] records: *Betty Cheapland, alias widow Adam, Craigyloch aged 74 years.*

Jane Brechin's mother, Jean Falconer, was resident in Laurencekirk at the time of the trial and execution of John Adam in 1835. There is a record of a *Widow Brechin* in the July 1835 Communion Roll of the Laurencekirk parish church[34] but there is no record of her after that date. There are no old parish registers of deaths/burials in Laurencekirk nor does she appear in the 1841 census[77], so it seems likely that she died between the July 1835 and July 1836 communions. She would have been aged 74 or 75. Jane's brother, Robert, married Margaret Daker in Garvock on 18 November 1809[13] but there seems to have been no children. There is some evidence that after Jean Falconer's death they moved to Glasgow, where Robert was a shoemaker. However, they appear to have separated. Margaret died of decline in Glasgow[79] on 5 August 1846, being recorded as *Mrs Margaret Brechin* (or Hamilton). Robert died of *debility* in Gorbals [Glasgow][79] on 16 April 1849, age 67, recorded as *Robert Brechen* [he was actually aged 64].

Jane Brechin had two sisters, Agnes and Mary. Agnes, her elder sister, married John Murray in Garvock on 3 August 1806[13]. There were nine children: William (1807), Margaret (1808), David (1809), Elizabeth (1811), Ann (1812), Mary (1813), Peter (1815) and Susan (1816) – all born in Garvock; and Alexander (1825), born in. Fordoun[80], a parish centred on the village of Auchenblae, north of Laurencekirk. Agnes died, age 51, of *influenza and water on the lung* on 30 January 1837 at the farm of Shepherdshaugh, Fordoun, recorded as *Agnes Brichen* [she was actually aged 53].

Jane Brechin's younger sister, Mary, married Archibald Gouk in Garvock on 8 June 1822[13]. They lived on Rossie Island in the parish of Craig, near Montrose, where Archibald worked a fourteen acre farm. They travelled to Inverness to identify Jane Brechin's body after the murder and Archibald gave evidence at the trial. They had nine children: Mary born illegitimately in Marykirk in 1819; and William (1824), Archibald (1825), David (1826), Agnes (1828), Jean (1830), James (1833), Robert (1834) and John (1839), all born on Rossie Island, parish of Craig, Angus. Archibald died at Rossie Island of *inflammation of the lungs* on 21 February 1858 and Mary continued farming with her unmarried daughter, Mary, and son, Robert, until she died there of diarrhoea on 18 September 1874, age 75. The certificate[78] records her father as *Robert Brechin, crofter*, and her mother as *Jane Brechin, maiden surname Falconer* [she was actually aged 78].

There is no record in Dingwall (or Inverness) of a child born to Dorothy Elliott and John Adam. On 21 May 1835, Sheriff Jardine of Ross & Cromarty indicated that his office had applied to Dorothy's home parish [Wirksworth] in Derbyshire to take her back. If Dorothy Elliott was pregnant at that time, the purpose of this application might have been to send Dorothy home to have her baby at her parents' house in St Mary's Gate, Wirksworth – where she and the baby would not be a burden on parish Poor Funds. When she visited John in Inverness Tolbooth on 27 May 1835 she may have known that she was returning to Derbyshire and needed to inform him that *until the result of the trial, she would no more visit him*. Whether she also took the opportunity to inform John that she was pregnant is not known. Although she was included in the list of summoned witnesses to the trial, she was not called to give evidence and there is no proof that she actually attended the trial on 18-19 September. Thus, it is possible that she did travel to Derbyshire to have her baby and only returned to Inverness four an a half months later to meet John Adam on 15 October, the eve of the execution. However, there is no record (either in the Wirksworth parish or non-conformist records)[23] of a child being born in that period. Thus, it has to be concluded that, if she was pregnant, the child either did not survive or was given to a 'baby farmer' for adoption.

Whether Dorothy returned to Wirksworth after the execution is not known. Her mother, Margery, seems to have died circa 1835-36 but her father was still alive in 1839 when, on 20 May, Dorothy married a colliery pitman named Robert Ferry in the Northumbrian parish of Long Benton[81] – in the northern outskirts of Newcastle. The marriage certificate gives Dorothy's age as 22 [she was actually 21, but only two and a half weeks short of 22] and names her father, Edward, and her sister, Jane, as witnesses.

The couple initially lived in the Killingworth Colliery cottages at Long Benton. [The Killingworth Colliery is where George Stephenson in 1814 built his first locomotive, *Blucher*.] In 1850, Robert and Dorothy moved to Shotton Colliery Village in Durham where a new mine had opened in 1841. By this time they had four children: Jane, born 1842; Alice, born 1844; Dorothy, born 1846; and Robert

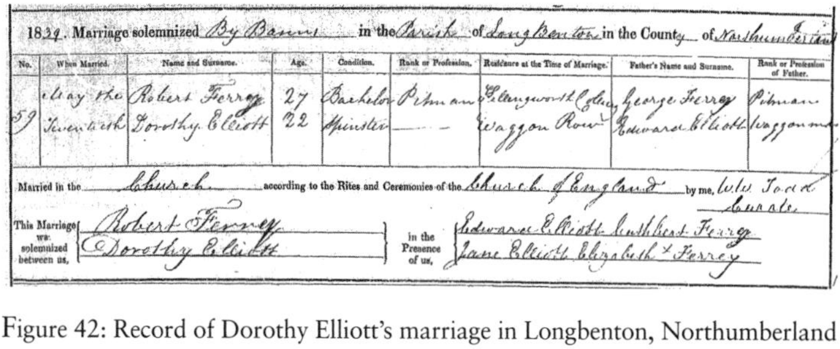

Figure 42: Record of Dorothy Elliott's marriage in Longbenton, Northumberland in May 1839 (General Register Office)

William, born 1849. By 1860 the family had moved to California Row, Seaham Colliery Pit Village and a fifth child had been added to the family: Edward, born in 1852 in Shotton. Seaham colliery was plagued by accidents and explosions and by 1870 Robert and Dorothy had returned to Shotton Colliery and were living in Chapel Row, Shotton. However, Shotton colliery closed in 1877 and they moved to Railway Terrace, West Cornforth, Stockton-on-Tees, Durham where Dorothy died on 29 March 1879, aged 61, of *chronic endocarditis*[82]. In 1871, her daughter, Dorothy, had presented her with a grand-daughter – also named Dorothy.

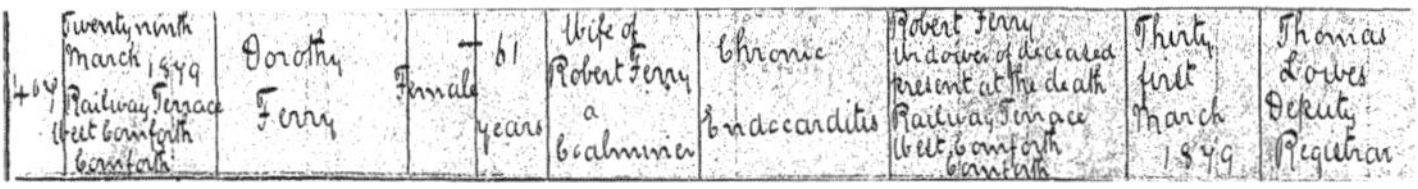

404	Twenty ninth March 1879 Railway Terrace West Cornforth Cornforth	Dorothy Ferry	Female	61 years	Wife of Robert Ferry a Coalminer	Chronic Endocarditis	Robert Ferry Widower of deceased present at the death Railway Terrace West Cornforth Cornforth	Thirty first March 1879	Thomas Lowes Deputy Registrar

Figure 43: Dorothy Elliott's death record in the Stockton, Durham register of deaths of March 1879 (General Register Office)

(vii) Jane's Endowment

When John Adam was arrested in April 1835 there was £74 in the black leather pocket book that was found under his pillow. There was also a receipt from John Macdonald for a £5 pre-payment and £20 security against the hire of a horse. This money was quickly recovered by Procurator-Fiscal Hugh Cameron and deposited in his name, along with the £74, in the National Bank in Dingwall. As one of the banknotes was a valueless John Maberly & Co 20/- note, the total deposit was £98 – a substantial sum in 1835, equivalent in spending power to *circa* £8000 today.

The issue of who was the legitimate heir to this money had been raised even before the trial commenced and the deliberations continued well after the execution. The evidence is in correspondence contained in the collections of the precognition[44] and trial[51] papers.

As early as 8 September 1835 the Procurator-Fiscal of Montrose, Robert Burness, wrote to the Crown Counsel, David Cleghorn, on behalf of Jane Brechin's family: *It having fallen to me to take the legal precognitions in this neighbourhood in the above case [John Adam or Anderson, Inverness Circuit], the friends of the deceased Jane Brechin have naturally applied to me for some assistance in securing for them the money of which their sister was deprived by the wicked devices of John Adam two days before their unhappy marriage.*

In the circumstances so unusual, I am at a loss how to advise the poor relatives, consisting of four sisters and a brother [actually, a mother, two sisters, a sister-in-law and a brother] but it occurs to me that in such a case Crown Counsel may be able and disposed so to arrange the matter at the trial, as the relatives may obtain their sister's money without being exposed to unnecessary trouble or expense. The amount taken out of Adam's custody on his apprehension at Dingwall was £74, one pound of which was a note of Maberly & Co. This sum, contained in a pocket book, I understand was sent to you along with precognition, and of course it still remains with you or with Crown Counsel. Besides this sum, a further £25 was recovered from a person of the name of MacDonald or Michael of Dingwall, which Adam had given him a day or two before his apprehension for the use of an entire horse for the season, and in security for its safe return at the end of that time. This latter sum was lodged in National Bank at Dingwall on deposit receipt in favour of Mr Cameron, the Procurator-Fiscal there, to abide the orders of the law, and the receipt forms part of the precognition. These two sums fall a little short of the amount belonging to the deceased and uplifted by Adam from the Banks here two days before the marriage, as will appear from the evidence of Mr Hill and Mr Beattie the agents here of the National Bank and the British Linen Co. Besides money, furniture and other effects belonging to the deceased were conveyed from this [place], and reached Adam's house at Dingwall, all of which should be restored to her relatives.

I fear I am presuming too far in addressing you on the subject of the private interests of the poor people to whom I refer, but under the peculiar circumstances of this case, probably you or the Crown Counsel may be pleased to say whether any measures should be adopted previous to or at the trial for securing the object in view.

This letter was sent in a package that also contained a short second letter. This was from the Provost of Montrose, John Barclay: *I beg leave respectfully to recommend the unfortunate relatives of the deceased Jane Brechin and Mr Burness's application on their behalf, to the favourable consideration of Crown Counsel.*

David Cleghorn passed these letters to Advocate-Depute John Shaw-Stewart, Lord Moncrieff, who responded on 12 September: *I have just received your letter of the 9 September forwarding to me letter from the Procurator-Fiscal at Montrose regarding the case of John Adam. I herewith enclose the letter and beg you will return to him the answer suggested by yourself, if necessary to send an answer. I do not know whether it might not be pertinent if possible to obtain from Adam an assignation to his property in favour of the relatives of his wife, which in the event of his conviction, might save questions both with the Crown and with his own relatives. Such a suggestion cannot come from us officially, and you may judge whether a hint to this effect could be given by you privately to Burness, who seems so much interested in the poor woman's relatives.*

Robert Burness seems to have received a reply to his letter to David Cleghorn next day [9 September] as it is acknowledged in a subsequent letter [of 28 September]. However, its contents are not recorded. Whether he ever received private correspondence after David Cleghorn had received advice from the Lord Advocate is also not recorded – neither is there any evidence that John Adam (or his defence counsel) was approached on the subject of providing an assignation, should he be found guilty. In any case, if John had been approached, it would have been quite out-of-character for him to accede to any such suggestion.

The full sentence ordained in writing by Lord Moncrieff after John's trial on 18 September had contained the clause: ... *all his moveable goods and gear to be escheat [confiscated] and inbrought to His Majesty's use.* In effect, this clause referred to Jane Brechin's 'goods and gear' because, in Scots law, all her possessions had transferred into the ownership of John Adam at the time of their marriage. However, there were complexities arising from John's co-habitation with Dorothy which challenged the validity of John's marriage to Jane – and therefore his ownership of the escheated possessions. It had been in an attempt to avoid these potentially intricate legal nuances that it had been suggested that John might be approached to issue an assignation of property to Jane's relations.

Knowing that John's money had been escheat to the Crown, John's defence solicitor Charles Stewart, submitted his claim for expenses to Lord Moncrieff on 21 September. The covering letter explained: *I use the freedom of enclosing an account of the expense incurred by me in the defence of John Adam at the late Circuit, and shall feel much obliged by your presenting the same to Exchequer in order to be paid out of the funds found in the custody of Pannel when apprehended. I understand the practice to be to transmit such accounts through the Crown Counsel acting on the Circuit. Mr Crawford declined to accept any fee.*

Although the defence counsel James Crawford did not claim any fee, his junior associate Edward Gordon had been paid four guineas for his attendance at the trial – an amount that was included in Charles Stewart's account[83] for the sum of £14-9-2d. Other items included in his account were: two days spent with John Adam, Defence Counsel and witnesses in Dingwall (£4-14-6d); gig hire and ferry charges (£1-1/-); various fees and copying (£1-3-8d); attendance at the trial (£3-3/-); and refreshments (3/-).

Rev Cook of Laurencekirk, who had officiated at John and Jane's marriage ceremony, had obviously been the driving force behind Procurator-Fiscal Burness's initial enquiries about Jane's money and other possessions. He clearly believed that his pastoral role on behalf of the Brechin family extended to doing everything possible to procure their moral right to Jane's money. To his credit, after John's trial, Rev Cook had sought out Lord Moncrieff to request advice and subsequently, on 26 September 1835, he informed Robert Burness: *I had some conversation with the Depute Advocate and the Procurator-Fiscal of Dingwall about the effects of the poor woman, Jane Brechin. The Advocate said he thought there would be willingness on the part of the Crown to favour the woman's relations by bestowing on them her effects, in so far as*

191

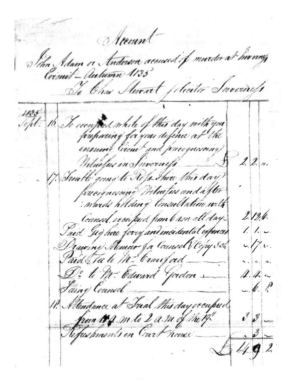

Figure 44: Charles Stewart's expenses claim for defending John Adam
at his trial in September 1835 (National Records of Scotland)

*these were escheated but there were two questions as to the Crown's
interest: even if the ceremony at Laurencekirk was a legal marriage, its
speedy dissolution would affect Adam's interest in her goods, but on the
evidence which was brought out on the trial it was considered that Adam
was virtually married to the girl Elliott and therefore could contract no
other matrimonial engagement. In this last case Jane Brechin's whole
effects would fall to her relations. Mr Shaw-Stewart finally [had come to
his opinion] that the friends had best make an application to the Crown
Agent in Edinburgh – which would lead to a consideration and final
determination by the Crown Authorities, and it was suggested that, as
you had already corresponded on the subject, and were not far distant*

from the friends, you might prepare the application in their name and have stated this (since my return today) to the friends here, who quite concur in the views, and from what passed between Gouk and me at Inverness I doubt not but he and his wife will also agree. The purpose of my writing you, you will therefore understand, and I hope you will find it convenient to give early attention to the matter.

Robert Burness transmitted this information to David Cleghorn on 28 September and requested advice on how the application on behalf of Jane's relations should be addressed: *I received the favour of your letter of 9th current, and felt much obliged by your attention. In reference to my letter to you of the 8th I beg leave to send you annexed a copy of a letter I have received from the Rev Cook of Laurencekirk, communicating an interview between him and the Depute Advocate Mr Shaw-Stewart, wherein it is suggested that the application referred to should be made to you. Whether it is meant that it should be made thro' you to the Crown Counsel or to the Lords of Treasury thro' you, I am not very certain, and I hope you will excuse the further trouble of suggesting the correct course to use.*

Meanwhile, in Edinburgh, the Lord Advocate [John Murray], Solicitor-General [John Cunninghame] and Advocate-Depute [John Shaw-Stewart, Lord Moncrieff] were exchanging notes on the validity of John Adam's marriage to Jane Brechin and on the conflicting rights of the Crown and Jane's heirs. On 10 October, the Advocate-Depute wrote a note to the Lord Advocate: *Adam was convicted at the last Inverness Circuit of the murder of Jane Brechin. He had a few weeks before the murder been married to her* in facie ecclesia, *and had obtained possession of money (above £100) and other moveables belonging to her. There is much ground to believe that he married her for the sole purpose of possessing himself of her property, and with the intention afterwards to murder her.*

Above a year before his marriage to Jane Brechin he had, on deserting from his Regiment in England, prevailed on Dorothy Elliott, by a promise of marriage, to accompany him to Scotland. He has never been formally married to her, but he lived with her under a complete habit and repute as man and wife for about a year in Dingwall. The nature and circumstances of his cohabitation with Dorothy Elliott as these appeared in the evidence at the trial, were such as to raise strong doubts whether she had not, by the Law of Scotland, acquired the status of his wife, and consequently whether the subsequent marriage with Jane Brechin was not invalid.

The relatives of Jane Brechin are now applying (as the accompanying letter shows) for the property which belonged to her. If the marriage with Jane Brechin be valid, then, I presume, the whole property is escheated to the Crown. But if it be invalid, it rather appears that it would fall to her heirs.

The Lord Advocate will consider, whether in the whole circumstances of the case, it may not be better to recommend that the Crown should give up, in favour of the heirs of the poor woman, all claim on this property under the forfeiture. Even supposing the right of Crown to be good, they have a strong claim – ie misericordia; But the right of the Crown seems to involve rather a nice and troublesome question, the discussion of which would thus be avoided. [Misericordia occurs in cases where there are two or more joint actions. In law one action requires one judgement, thus no single judgement can be made to several joint actions. Misericordia gives a judge 'mercy' to use discretion in reaching a verdict in such cases.]

The Agent who conducted the defence of Adam, has handed to me an account of his expenses with an application for payment out of these funds. The view to be taken of this application may in some measure depend on opinion which the Lord Advocate may be able to form on the point of law above noticed. The Agent's letter and account will be found among the papers of the case.

Having given due consideration to these issues, on 22 October the Lord Advocate wrote a note to the Solicitor-General containing some further thoughts on which he wished to consult: *This is a case of considerable nicety and with regard to which Lord Advocate was to confer with Solicitor General.*

The 1st point is whether the marriage with Jane Brechin in 'facie Ecclesiae' *was valid. The doubt here arises from his having cohabited with Dorothy Elliott under a promise of marriage made in England. This is a very nice question, but in the whole circumstances, I am inclined to think that the marriage with Jean Brechin is to be presumed a legal marriage. Lord Moncrieff however is said to have expressed privately a different opinion and that a cohabitation marriage is good in such circumstances.*

2 – Supposing he was married to Jane Brechin, the one half of the property would be escheated to the Crown and the other would belong to her relations.

3 – Supposing him not the husband of Jane Brechin and that the marriage was null and void in consequence of his previous marriage, then money and moveables he had obtained from Jane Brechin was on false pretences as being her husband when he was not. In that case it would be the property of Jean Brechin and go to her relations.

4 – There is another question whether when a prisoner has money in his possession which he is not charged with having stolen, the money should be applied in conducting his defence although it may afterwards appear that he acquired it by fraud. This may also require consideration, but I am rather inclined to think that the whole ought to be given up to the woman's friends.

Whilst the legal discussions on the disposition of Jane's money were being pursued, Charles Stewart's account remained unpaid. Probably still under the belief that the Crown had confiscated Jane's money and having awaited payment for over a month, he re-submitted his account on 26 October, together with a formal declaration, taken by Provost Smith JP, of his role as John Adam's agent: *Compeared Charles Stewart solicitor in Inverness who being solemnly sworn and examined, depones that he was employed as Agent in the defence of John Adam or Anderson accused of murder at the last Autumn Circuit in Inverness and whose effects were escheat to the Crown in consequence of the conviction – that the foregoing account amounting to fourteen pounds nine shillings and two pence Sterling [£14-9-2d] was incurred to the deponent as Agent aforesaid and that no part thereof has been paid or compensated in any manner of way. All of which he depones to be truth as he shall answer to God. Robert Smith JP.*

A week later, still having no response to the submission of his account[83], Charles Stewart engaged Campbell & Traill WS to pursue his claim. [WS refers to 'Writers to the Signet' who were senior solicitors who had special privileges in relation to the drawing up of certain types of document which required the Royal signet (seal). These no longer exist and the post-nominal letters WS now refer to a member of the Society of Writers – an independent, non-regulatory association of Scottish solicitors.]

Campbell & Traill WS wrote to the Lord Advocate on 3 November: *We have been applied to by Mr Charles Stewart, Writer in Inverness, to bring under your Lordship's notice his claim for payment of an account of £14-9-2 incurred by him in the defence of John Adam or Anderson lately convicted at the Inverness Circuit for the murder of Jane Brechin. When Adam was apprehended about £100 were found in his possession and is now in the hands of the Procurator-Fiscal of Inverness-shire. The account was, when incurred, furnished to Mr Shaw-Stewart and, we understand, was by him submitted to your Lordship. We now take the liberty of enclosing a duplicate of the account with affidavit by Mr Charles Stewart [see 26 Oct]. It will be observed that the greater part of it is for fees to Counsel and expense in precognosing witnesses and we beg respectfully to express our hope that your Lordship will give the claim your favourable consideration and order payment of it from the funds above alluded to. Mr Charles Stewart undertook the employment with great reluctance and only on the distinct understanding that he would be paid out of the prisoner's funds.*

On 18 November, Rev Cook decided to write directly to David Cleghorn, rather than through the medium of Robert Burness. There is a hint of frustration and irascibility in his words: *James Brechin [erroneous – his name was Robert], the only brother of the unfortunate woman Jane Brechin for whose murder Adam was lately executed at Inverness, resides in Laurencekirk alongwith the mother and a sister [actually a sister-in-law, Robert's wife], and a few days ago applied to me to know if any management had been made as to his sister's effects, as to which a statement was, I believe, forwarded to you. In these circumstances, I hope you will excuse my troubling you about this matter, on behalf of friends, especially as to those of them who are my parishioners and who are very poor, their share of the effects will be very serviceable. May I then beg of you to have the goodness to inform me whether the Crown Advisers have so far considered the representation made on behalf of the friends, as to have come to any determination regarding it?*

Under his right to make a discretionary judgement in the spirit of *misericordia*, the Lord Advocate finally issued his opinion on the matter of the validity of the marriage (and therefore the disbursement of Jane's money and the payment of Charles Stewart's account). In his note of 9 December, he clearly had decided that it was best to forsake the Crown's rights of escheat in favour of an even-handed position on the claims of Jane's relatives and John's defence solicitor: *It appears to me that Adam must be considered as married to the person he afterwards murdered. The marriage having been a regular one, I doubt whether he was married to the other person, and even if he was so, the other marriage in absence of all legal proceedings must be held to be good. In these circumstances the one half of the effects belong at once to the wife's relations and the other half ought to be given to them after paying the necessary expenses of his defence, as the forfeiture can only operate from the period of sentence and these expenses ought to have been paid before. They, however, ought to be limited as much as possible to the necessary outlay and a moderate fee to the Junior Counsel to defray the expense of his journey to the north. Mr Stewart, who was Clerk on the Northern Circuit at the trial, can audit and certify the expenses to be allowed on this principle. The account given in by the Agent seems to contain some charges which should be checked and modified.*

The Lord Advocate's opinion was transmitted to Robert Burness by David Cleghorn on 16 December: *Referring to my former letters to you as to the application of the friends of Jane Brechin regarding the effects of this person, I have now to inform you that Lord Advocate has issued a note on this subject, of which I beg leave to send you a copy prefixed. I would suggest, therefore, that you should now get a petition to Lords of Treasury, prepared on behalf of Jane Brechin's relations, stating the circumstances and forward it to the Treasury, where I hope it may meet with a favourable reception.*

David Cleghorn's release of the Lord Advocate's opinion received an immediate and somewhat indignant response from Robert Burness. He had good reason – in his well-meaning even-handedness, the Lord Advocate had made Jane Brechin's relatives liable for the payment of John Adam's defence. The response, dated 17 December, states: *I am this morning favoured with your letter of yesterday, with copy note of the 9th [December] by the Lord Advocate and I am afraid relations of the unfortunate Jane Brechin will be much disappointed to find that his Lordship entertains the opinion that they are liable for the expense of conducting the defence of the murder of their late sister, or what is the same thing, so far as they are concerned, that it must be paid not from Adam's own funds, if he had any, but out of that money of which he wickedly defrauded her a few weeks before her death.*

It humbly occurs to me that his Lordship has overlooked one circumstance which may yet materially affect his opinion upon that point. He holds the last marriage as good in the absence of all legal proceedings, and from that circumstance infers that one half of the effects belongs at once to the wife's relations, and that the other half ought to be given to them. No doubt holding the marriage to be good and that it had subsisted for a year and a day, only one half as a matter of right, would have fallen to the wife's relations, but in this instance, the marriage did not subsist for a year and a day, and had John Adam been alive, he must have restored not one half, but the whole of those funds which he obtained from his wife on the occasion of her marriage. The moment of her death rendered full restitution exigible from him, and whatever he received became a debt by him to her Executors, subject to no abatement of his future contractions. The amount which he received is clearly defined by the precognitions, and the money, on Adam's apprehension, to the amount of £98, was secured and placed under the charge of the officers of the Crown – and I am sure the relatives of the deceased, who are respectable but poor people, must feel disappointed if that sum be not restored to them without abatement. If you think proper you may have the goodness to submit these observations to the Lord Advocate, and I should wish to see a copy of the account claimed for the defence.

On receipt of Robert Burness's response next day, 18 December, David Cleghorn copied it to the Lord Advocate with a covering note: *The Crown Agent communicated the order of Lord Advocate as to the disposal of the property found on this man [John Adam] to Robert Burness, Procurator-Fiscal Montrose by letter, of which a copy is herewith sent.*

The Crown Agent this day received a letter from Robert Burness requesting the Lord Advocate to reconsider his opinion so far as it applies to the expenses of the prisoner's defence. The Crown Agent is not certain whether the point of law stated by Mr Burness was under the view of the Lord Advocate and Solicitor-General when they disposed of this case.

On 21 December, realising that he had inadvertently made an error of judgement, the Lord Advocate annotated David Cleghorn's note: *The marriage having been dissolved within a year and a day as very properly pointed out by Mr Burness, the whole fund belongs to the wife's relations and should be returned to them.*

This revised judgement, however, was highly unfavourable to Charles Stewart who now had no means of recovering either his own expenses as defence solicitor or the fees that he had, in good faith, paid to the junior defence counsel, Edward Gordon. His tactic was now to cajole John Jardine, Sheriff of Ross & Cromarty, to take up his cause. John Jardine seems to have consulted the Solicitor-General and subsequently wrote to David Cleghorn on 27 December: *I have just seen the Solicitor-General who tells me that you are in course of taking measures for the appropriation of the money belonging to the unfortunate woman, Jane Brechin, who was murdered at Millbuie ... and at his suggestion I write this note to you to request that you will not proceed further in the business for a day or two until the opinion of Crown Counsel be taken as to certain claims on this fund which I attach to this letter [Charles Stewart's expenses].*

John Jardine's letter to David Cleghorn was quickly followed up by another from Campbell & Frail WS on 29 December: *On 3 December we had the honour of addressing the Lord Advocate on the subject of a claim by the Agent (Mr Charles Stewart) who was employed in the defence of John Adam, convicted at the last Inverness Circuit for the murder of Jane Brechin, and we transmitted to his Lordship a duplicate of the account with affidavit by Mr Stewart, in the hope that he would consider the claim favourably and order payment of it (£14-2-9) from the funds which were found on Adams on his apprehension. The Lord Advocate was pleased to express his willingness to consider the claim favourably, but until the matter was settled whether the money belongs to Adam's relations, he could make no order on our application.*

On a communication we lately had with the Lord Advocate's Clerk, we regretted to learn that there was a probability of this claim being rejected. We trust however that this will not be the case and that it is not yet too late to have it reconsidered. With this view we now take the liberty to enclose a letter we yesterday received from Mr Stewart on the subject and request you will have the goodness to draw the attention of the Crown Counsel to the justice of Stewart's claim as well as to the impolicy of refusing remuneration to an Agent under such circumstances.

On receipt of this letter pointing out the unfairness of the final judgement, David Cleghorn sent a note to the Lord Advocate on 7 January 1836: *Messrs Campbell & Traill WS who wrote to the Lord Advocate as to a claim by Mr Stewart, solicitor in Inverness, for payment of expenses incurred by him in defending John Adam, have written to the Crown Agent sending a letter from their correspondent on the subject.*

As this property was disposed of by the Lord Advocate's direction of 21 December last, the Crown Agent submits that the Lord Advocate may now direct him to write Messrs Campbell & Traill stating that his Lordship cannot recommend any part of the expense of conducting the defence being paid out of the money found on Adam, which he holds belonged to the deceased Jean Brechin and now to her relations.

This final note in the collection is annotated: Letter sent to Campbell & Traill on 23 January 1836. It therefore has to be assumed that the Lord Advocate was unwilling to reconsider and authorised David Cleghorn to confirm his judgement to Campbell & Traill WS. Charles Stewart's account for acting as John Adam's defence solicitor therefore remained unpaid by the Exchequer. As John Adam had no money, it probably never was.

(viii) Jane's final Resting Place

Evidence from the precognition papers[44] and entries in the Dingwall parish treasurer's accounts[45] suggest that Jane Brechin was interred on Thursday 16 April 1835 within the graveyard of St Clement's parish church, Dingwall. No kirk session minutes or old parish registers of deaths or burials, have survived from this time, so there is no known record of the interment. However, a survey of the gravestones in St Clement's churchyard[84] has revealed a facing pair of small stones marking each end of a lair located on the west side of the church, 2.5 m apart, each engraved 'JB 1837'. It seems highly probable that these stones mark the final resting place of Jane Brechin and that the 1837 date refers, not to her date of death, but to the date on which the gravestones were erected.

According to the Lord Advocate's direction of 21 December 1835, the money found on John Adam was declared to belong to Jane Brechin. Thus, although there is no documentary evidence, Jane's money would have been given to her nearest blood relation, her mother. However, it seems probable that Jane's mother died between July 1835 and July 1836, so the money would eventually have come to Jane's three surviving siblings – Agnes, Robert and Mary. They, presumably, decided to use some of the money to erect the pair of memorial stones in Dingwall. It is quite probable that it would have taken them until 1837 to locate the lair and gain the necessary permissions – hence the date inscribed on the stones.

There is one final irony to the story of the murder of Jane Brechin. Jane's £98 legacy was earned from her successful grocery business. Part of that legacy paid for her memorial stones in St Clement's churchyard, Dingwall. Today that churchyard borders with Dingwall's most successful grocery – the Tesco supermarket.

Figure 45: Jane Brechin's gravestone in St Clement's
graveyard adjacent to Tesco's supermarket in Dingwall

NOTES, BIBLIOGRAPHY and REFERENCES

Key:

NRS – National Records of Scotland (previously the National Archives of Scotland), Edinburgh

NLS – National Library of Scotland, Edinburgh

HCA – Highland Archive Service (previously Highland Council Archives), Inverness

GRO – General Record Office (England & Wales)

GROS – General Record Office for Scotland, Edinburgh

TNA – The National Archives, Kew, London

CHAPTER 1

1. In Scotland, pre-1855 births, baptisms, marriages and deaths were recorded by Church of Scotland or Roman Catholic Church in Scotland parish ministers (or clerks) in what are now called the Old Parish Registers (OPR). The registers are held at the Scottish Records Office under the reference NRS CH2 – but digital images can be downloaded through the subscription web-site www. scotlandspeople.gov.uk. The earliest records date from 1538 (1703 for Catholic records) but many parishes did not commence their registers until the 18th century. The genealogical information recorded in the OPR is highly variable; for example some birth/baptism records do not name the child's mother and many parishes did not record deaths.

2. Lintrathen Old Parish Registers [NRS CH2/302/1-3].

3. In Scotland, wills and testaments had to be confirmed in the Commissary Court that had jurisdiction over the parish in which the person died. Wills and testaments made in Angus (Forfarshire) from 1549 are held in the Registers of Testaments of the Commissariots of Brechin, Dunkeld or St Andrews. Commissary Courts were abolished in 1823 and Sheriff Courts assumed responsibility for confirmation of testaments from 1 January 1824. Indexes and digital images are available at www.scotlandspeople.gov.uk.

4. The Airlie Muniments [NRS GD16] comprise three volumes. Vol I, Section 3 contains papers relating to estate ownership, heritable bonds and inventories of writs; Vol III, Section 49 contains papers relating to schoolmasters' salaries.

5. The Phrenological Journal and Miscellany, Vol 9, Article IX (1836). Rev Francis Cannan's account of John Adam's early life in Lintrathen is on pages 648-51 (see also reference 66).

6. Alison Mitchell (ed), *Pre-1855 Monumental Inscriptions in Angus, Vol. 1: Strathmore*, Scottish Genealogy Society (1993) lists the pre-1855 Memorial Inscriptions of gravestones in Lintrathen parish churchyard.

7. Timothy Pont, Map 29, *Middle Strathmore* (1580-90). William Roy, Map C.9.b 18, *Military Survey of Scotland* (1747-52). Digital images are available at www. nls/maps.

8. Lintrathen Kirk Session minutes [NRS CH2/243/3].

9. Oathlaw Kirk Session minutes [NRS CH2/287/6] and Book of Discipline [CH2/287/7].

CHAPTER 2

10. St Cyrus (Ecclesgreig) Old Parish Registers [NRS CH2/267/1-4].

11. William Garden, *A map of Kincardineshire* (1797). A digital image is available at www.nls/maps.

12. Montrose Old Parish Registers [NRS CH2/312/1-14].

13. Garvock Old Parish Registers [NRS CH2/260/1-2].

14. Marykirk Old Parish Registers [NRS CH2/265/1-3].

15. St Cyrus (Ecclesgreig) Kirk Session minutes [NRS CH2/590/1].

16. Gershom Cumming (engraver), *Forfarshire Illustrated* (1848).

17. Great Reform Act Plans and Reports (1832), Montrose, map 50; Report of the Burgh, pg 63. Digital images of the plan and the report are available at www. nls/maps.

18. Royal Burgh of Montrose, Town Council minutes (1825-31). Angus Archives [GB618 M/1/1/12].

CHAPTER 3

19. Aberdeen Sheriff Court; Record of Criminal Jury Trials [NRS SC1/55/8,9] and Minute Book of Summary Trials [NRS SC1/59/1].

20. Chapel of Garioch Kirk Session Treasurer's accounts [NRS CH2/527/5/97].

21. Chapel of Garioch Old Parish Registers [NRS CH2/179/1-2].

22. John Adam's army service records seem not to have survived. However, he is listed in the pay and muster rolls of the 2nd Dragoon Guards [TNA WO 12/157 & 158].

23. In England, indexes to pre-1837 parish records of births, marriages and deaths can be searched through several subscription web-sites, for example: www. findmypast.co.uk, www.thegenealogist.co.uk and www.ancestry.co.uk. Copies of actual parish records can to be purchased from county archives. There is an excellent portal to the baptisms, marriages, burials, censuses and many other Wirksworth parish records (1600 – 1900) at www.wirksworth.org.uk.

24. Register of Births and Baptisms at High Bridge Meeting, Newcastle, Northumberland (1762-1837) [RG8/86/105]. Digital images of pre-1837 non-conformist records are available at the subscription site www.bmdregisters.co.uk.

25. Soke and Wapentake of Wirksworth, Great Barmote Court verdicts & jury lists, Derbyshire County Archives [D163/3/1].

26. Description Return of a Deserter, Nottingham (1834) [NRS AD14/35/19/232].

27. War Office, Register of Army Deserters (1811-52) [TNA WO 25/2910].

28. War Office, Register of Captured Deserters (1833-36) [TNA WO 25/2944].

29. Dundee General Kirk Session minutes [NRS CH2/1218/10].

30. John Wood, *Plan of the Town of Dingwall from actual survey* (1821). A digital image is available at www.nls/maps.

31. Jonathan McColl, *Register of Electors of the Burgh of Dingwall 1832-42*; transcript of electoral rolls subsequent to 1832 Reform Act (1994) [HCA BDW/12/1/1].

CHAPTER 4

32. Dingwall Kirk Session Poor Roll Account [NRS CH2/711/4].
33. Laurencekirk Old Parish Registers [NRS CH2/263/1-2].
34. Laurencekirk Parish Church Communion Rolls for 1835-39 [CH2/939/17-19].
35. John Mitchell (ed), *Angus & Mearns Almanack and Commercial & Agricultural Remembrancer* (1835).
36. Reports of the Commissioners for Highland Roads and Bridges, Vols I-III (1802-63) [HCA CRC2/1/2].

CHAPTER 5

37. Back issues of Scottish local newspapers are generally available on microfilm at local reference libraries. Few have been indexed, however a useful guide to those that have been indexed can be found at www.nls.uk/collections/newspapers/indexes/index.cfm. Indexes to the *Inverness Journal* and the *Inverness Courier* are searchable at www.ambaile.org.uk/en/newspapers. The British Library's 19th century British newspapers database can be searched at the subscription site http://newspapers.bl.uk/blcs. This includes the *Caledonian Mercury* (Edinburgh), the *Aberdeen Journal* and the *Glasgow Herald*. The British Newspaper archive is searchable at the subscription site www.britishnewspaperarchive.co.uk. This includes several other Scottish titles. Some national titles also have searchable archives, for example *The Times* at http://archive.timesonline.co.uk/tol/archive and *The Scotsman* at www.archive.scotsman.com.
38. Petition to carry out post-mortem and take witness statements [NRS JC26/1835/126(29)].
39. Murder handbill [NRS JC26/1835/126(53)].
40. Petition to detain John Adam [NRS JC26/1835/126(28)].
41. Warrants for Transmission [HCA L/INV/HC/14/18/32].
42. Report of the Justices of the Peace of the County of Ross on the state of Ross-shire jails (1829) [NRS GD1/946/20].
43. Minute Book of the Burgh of Dingwall (1832-39) [Dingwall Museum 1/1/5].

CHAPTER 6

44. Precognition papers [NRS AD14/35/19]. The collection contains 427 pages of petitions, letters and witness declarations covering the period April to August 1835.
45. Dingwall (St Clement's) Parish Treasurer's Accounts [NRS CH2/711/18].
46. G. Campbell Smith, *Sketch of the Site of Ground about the House in which the Dead Body of Jane Brechin was found on the 10th April 1835* [Private communication].
47. Peter Brown, *Reduced Plan of the Survey of the Commons of Mulbuy, Cromarty, etc* (1816) [NRS RHP 4045]. A digital image is available at www.scotlandsplaces.gov.uk.
48. Digital images of Ordnance Survey 1, 6 and 25 inch/mile maps (1843-1961) are available at www.nls/maps.
49. Schedule of Precognition [NRS JC26/1835/126/32].

50. George Taylor and Andrew Skinner, *Survey and maps of the roads of North Britain or Scotland* (1776); Plate 3 shows the Inverness gibbet and Plate 31 shows the Jeally Brans Inn. Digital images are available at www.nls/maps.

CHAPTER 7

51. Trial papers [NRS JC26/1835/126]. The collection contains 58 items, dated mainly from August 1835 to January 1836. Several items are copies of letters and documents that are also duplicated in the precognition papers (see reference 44).
52. King's Letter of Diligence [NRS JC26/1835/126/16].
53. Indictment against John Adam [NRS JC26/1835/126/22].
54. John Adam's defence [NRS JC26/1835/126/9].
55. Inverness Circuit Court of Justiciary Minute Book, September 1835, [NAS JC11/83, pages 91v-94].
56. List of Assize [NRS JC26/1835/126/10].
57. Bank deposit receipts [NRS JC26/1835/126/1-3].
58. Craig Quarry employment record for John Adam [NRS JC26/1835/126/23].
59. Inverness Burgh Treasurer's Accounts [HCA BI/2/1/6].

CHAPTER 8

60. High Court Death Warrant [HCA L/INV/HC/12/30].
61. A.F. Young, *The Encyclopaedia of Scottish Executions (1750-1963)*, pages 31-32 (1998).
62. John Home, *A Plan of the River Ness with Banks and Lands adjacent* (1774). A digital image is available at www.ambaile.org.uk.
63. Inverness Burgh Treasurer's Accounts (1835) [HCA BI/2/1/5 and BI/2/1/6].
64. Inverness Jail Accounts (1835) [HCA PA/IB/TA 16(23a)].

CHAPTER 9

65. John Sutherland trial papers [HCA L/INV/HC/10/84].
66. *Case of John Adam, executed at Inverness, on the 16th October 1835, for the murder of his wife*, in The Phrenological Journal and Miscellany, Vol 9 (Sept 1834 – March 1836), Article IX, pages 644-656 (1836).
67. George Combe, *Application of Phrenology to the purposes of the 'Guarantee Society'* in The Phrenological Journal and Magazine of Moral Science, Vol LXIX, pages 297-310 (1841).
68. *Death Masks and Life Masks of the Famous and Infamous* in Scotland's Cultural Heritage Exhibition, University of Edinburgh (1988). Available from British Library, Boston Spa, West Yorkshire.
69. Scottish National Portrait Gallery [PGL 2117].
70. John Noble, *The Mulbuie Murder; Life and Trial of John Adam*. National Library of Scotland, History & Archaeology Pamphlet, 25(8), (1888).
71. Inverness Burgh Council minutes [HCA BI/1/1/18].
72. Inverness Prison Board minutes [HCA/CI/1/3/1].
73. The copy of John Noble's booklet (see 70) annotated by Deputy Chief Constable William Dalgleish in 1943 is in the Historical Display Cabinet at the

current headquarters of Northern Constabulary, Inverness.

74. James Curtis, *The Mysterious Murder of Maria Marten* (1828).

75. *Remarkable Trials; Case of John Adam for Murder* in the Legal Observer (or Journal of Jurisprudence), Vol 11, Supplement for March, 415-7 (1836).

76. Colin Sutherland, The Story of John Adam: The Mulbuie Murderer (1999) [HCA D1164/2].

77. Decennial national censuses containing genealogical data commenced in 1841. In Scotland, a '100-year rule' (currently) protects data from censuses after 1911. Digital images of enumeration book pages for the censuses between 1841 and 2011 are available at the subscription site www.scotlandspeople.gov.uk. For the 1841 census, there is complete coverage of all Scottish parishes at www.freecen.org.uk.

78. Statutory registration of births, marriages and deaths in Scotland commenced in 1855. Searchable indexes to the records and images are available at the subscription site www.scotlandspeople.gov.uk. Each record has a unique GROS reference, consisting of the registration district number (usually the parish), the registration book number (if any) and the entry number, for example the GROS reference for: the death of Helen Ogilvie in Kirriemuir is 299/00/0059 (1902); for the marriage of John Adam (jnr) in Glenisla is 290/00/0006 (1858); the death of John Adam (jnr) in Alyth is 328/0A/0021 (1900); and the death of Mary Gouk in Craig is 280/00/0035 (1874).

79. Glasgow Old Parish Registers [NRS CH2/644/1-2].

80. Fordoun Old Parish Registers [NRS CH2/259/1].

81. Statutory registration of births, marriages and deaths in England commenced in 1837. Searchable quarterly indexes to the records are available at several subscription sites, for example www.findmypast.co.uk, www.thegenealogist.co.uk and www.ancestry.co.uk. These provide only the volume and page numbers of the record index books. Copies of the records themselves can either be purchased through the web-sites, from county registry offices or from the GRO. Dorothy Elliott's marriage in 1839 is indexed in Northumberland County 1st quarter, Tynemouth Registration District, Vol 25, Page 443.

82. Indexed in Durham County 2nd quarter (1874), Stockton Registration District, Vol 10A, page 61.

83. Account to Charles Stewart, solicitor, Inverness [NRS JC26/1835/126/37].

84. Highland Family History Society, *Monumental Inscriptions, St Clement's Churchyard, Dingwall*, Section 7 (West side), no 94.